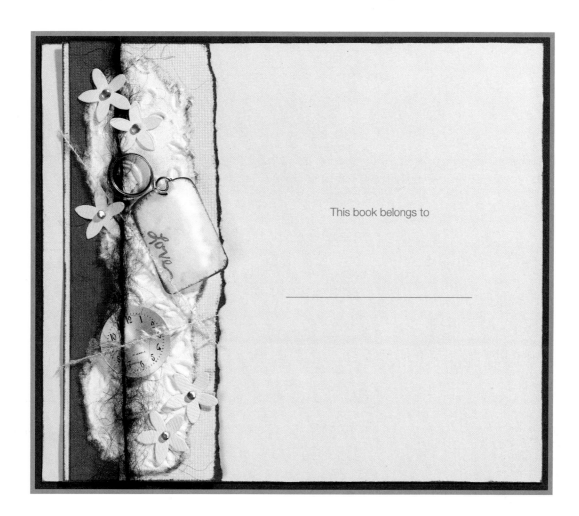

This book belongs to

_____

We dedicate this book to our Memory Makers contributors whose wonderful
pages serve as inspiration for giving special distinction to adult years in scrapbooks.

Table of Contents

This Is Me
12-29

Sure-to-inspire scrapbook pages all about self-celebration. Discover different ways to design introspective scrapbook pages that are every bit as unique as you are. Who knew turning the camera and page-creating process on yourself could be so rewarding and so much fun?

Love Stories
30-49

Lovely love-inspired layouts that pay tribute to those who melt your heart. These pull-at-your-heartstrings pages will leave you reeling with ideas for ways to record your one-of-a-kind romance. Not even Cupid himself could craft designs as divine as these.

Family Matters
50-69

Fantastic approaches for featuring your favorite familial faces. Enjoy eye-catching compositions that capture notorious family "characters," classic family moments and meaningful family memories. Revisiting relatives in your album is the next-best-thing to that rowdy family reunion.

Scrapbooking your Adult Years

185 outstanding ideas for pages about grown-ups

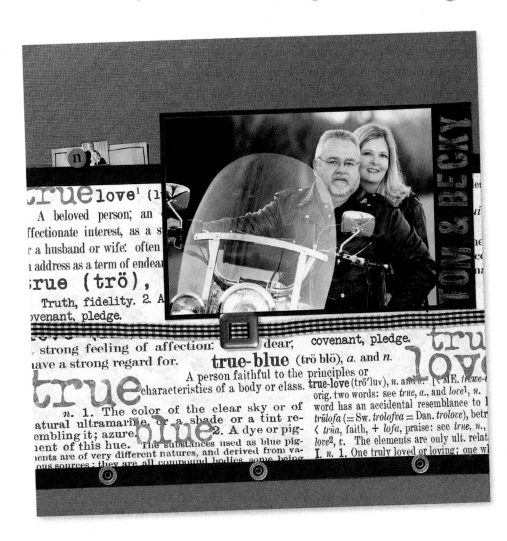

Executive Editor Kerry Arquette   *Founder* Michele Gerbrandt

Editor Emily Curry Hitchingham

Art Director Andrea Zocchi

Designer Nick Nyffeler

Art Acquisitions Editor Janetta Abucejo Wieneke

Craft Editor Jodi Amidei

Photographer Ken Trujillo

Contributing Photographers Brenda Martinez, Terry Ownby, Ruth Ann Praska, Jennifer Reeves

Art Caption Writer Nicole Cummings

Editorial Support Karen Cain, MaryJo Regier, Lydia Rueger, Dena Twinem

Memory Makers® Scrapbooking Your Adult Years

Published by Memory Makers Books, an imprint of F+W Publications, Inc.

12365 Huron Street, Suite 500, Denver, CO 80234

Phone 1-800-254-9124

First edition. Printed in the United States.

08 07 06 05 04 5 4 3 2 1

Library of Congress Cataloging-in-Publication Data

Scrapbooking your adult years : 175 outstanding ideas for pages about grown-ups.--1st
     p. cm
  Includes index.
  ISBN 1-892127-41-5
  1. Photograph albums. 2. Photographs--Conservation and restoration. 3. Scrapbooks. I.
Memory Makers Books.

TR465.S3945 2004
745.593--dc22

2004047563

Distributed to trade and art markets by

F+W Publications, Inc.

4700 East Galbraith Road, Cincinnati, OH 45236

Phone 1-800-289-0963

ISBN 1-892127-41-5

Memory Makers Books is the home of *Memory Makers*, the scrapbook magazine dedicated to educating and inspiring scrapbookers. To subscribe, or for more information, call 1-800-366-6465.
Visit us on the Internet at www.memorymakersmagazine.com.

You've Gotta Have Friends
70-87

Terrific page ideas that pay homage to the comrades, confidants and companions that are with us through thick and thin. These creative concepts give new cause for focusing on the fortune found in friendships. Here you'll find new ways to lavish artistic attention on your most tried-and-true fans.

Just For Fun
88-105

Wonderful ways for recording how you choose to unwind and spend your "spare" time. See how you can showcase your special interests, activities and enthusiasms in pages that pin down your passions and focus exclusively on fun. Explore inspiring examples for featuring life after work and grown-up responsibilities.

More Than A Job
106-123

Outstanding examples for expressing what your occupation means to you. Look to these layouts to help determine innovative ways to document the rewards of 9-to-5 life and military service that reflect your on-the-job pride, diligence and dedication.

My One True Love

I AM SO VERY LUCKY TO HAVE FOUND
MY BEST FRIEND AND BE ABLE TO SHARE
MY LIFE WITH HIM. WE'VE BEEN MARRIED
FOR OVER A DECADE NOW AND THERE HAVE
CERTAINLY BEEN TIMES OF UPS AND DOWNS.
OVER THE YEARS WE'VE HAD THREE CHILDREN
AND WITH A TREMENDOUS AMOUNT OF HARD
WORK, WE HAVE SUCCESSFULLY STARTED A
BUSINESS OF OUR OWN. THROUGH IT ALL
OUR LOVE HAS REMAINED STRONG. WE'VE
LEARNED TO COMMUNICATE, MAKE COMPROMISES,
AND SUPPORT EACH OTHER IN WHATEVER WE DO.
AND NOW AT THIS TIME IN OUR LIVES,
WHEN WE LOOK AHEAD AT THIS JOURNEY WE
CALL LIFE, I'M GLAD THAT I CAN SHARE THIS
TIME WITH MY BEST FRIEND.

Introduction

Becoming "grown-ups" means we cross into a unique phase of life. The carefree days of adolescence seem distant as we face the routine realities of every day...bills, careers, carpools and "what's for dinner?" quandaries. While becoming a grown-up may have once seemed like the-stop-where-fun-got-off, it turns out on the road of life, our adult years are ever-evolving times of self-discovery, accomplishments and milestones. Around each bend is a fresh challenge and rewarding experience and in each passing year is newfound wisdom upon which to reflect.

Like many scrapbookers, you have most likely devoted yourself to recording the lives and times of others. In particular, new births and growing children are constant muses for filling many albums. However, much less prevalent and equally important are scrapbook pages that celebrate what it is to be the one behind the camera and beyond the growing-up years. It's time there was a resource for scrapbookers that features grown-ups enjoying their grown-up lives.

Scrapbooking Your Adult Years is just such a tool. Inside you'll find page after page of innovative artwork starring adults—from pages showcasing special friendships and romantic relationships, to those commemorating the role of work, the fun of play and the love of families. These never-before-seen pages will leave you reeling with ideas for adult-driven layouts with their artful approaches and outstanding composition. You'll be motivated to put your own creative touches on the cutting-edge techniques and designs featured, inspiring you to document your own unique memories based on what you'll see inside. Additionally, you'll discover tips for time-efficient scrapbooking and helpful lists of potential page ideas.

We may be all grown up, but never should our responsibilities and obligations keep us from creating incredible memories from countless good times—and from having a little fun. You can never grow out of that.

Michele

Michele Gerbrandt
Founding Editor
Memory Makers magazine

Tips for time-efficient scrapbooking

Although grown-up life provides plenty of scrapbook-worthy moments, milestones and memories, finding time to record them in your scrapbook is not an easy task. Sometimes the very creativity it takes to make a layout is required for fina-gling scrapbooking opportunities in our hectic grown-up schedules. Make the most of what time you do have by putting these strategies to work so you have more time to play.

Determine if you are a night owl or a rise-with-the-sun-scrapbooker. Your productivity is directly tied to your time of peak creative performance. Pinpoint when you are most likely to be energized and uninterrupted throughout the day and claim a portion of that time for crafting.

Identify windows of opportunity that arise in your schedule. Take advantage of your children's nap time, those minutes when dinner is in the oven, or while watching those just-can't-miss television programs to chip away at your works-in-progress. Repurpose idle time such as substituting an hour of channel or Web surfing for an hour of scrap-booking for a surefire way to fill albums in a flash.

Scribble down spur-of-the-moment page ideas. Sometimes those stop-you-in-your-tracks ideas sneak up at the most unexpected moments. Be ready to record them by carrying a few index cards or a small notebook with you for when divine inspiration strikes. Additionally, sketch page ideas while waiting for doctor appointments to utilize time and all those magazines at your disposal for idea inspiration. In doing so, you are mounting an arsenal of ready ideas for times when creativity is stalled.

Commit yourself to a scrapbooking calendar. Custom-design a creative agenda so that you scrapbook on a regular basis. In setting aside predetermined dates, you are more apt to finish your layouts in a timely fashion and can plan ahead for future projects.

Set page-completion goals. Whether five or twenty-five, focus on finishing a select number of pages each month to ensure a steady scrapbooking pace. For added incentive, reward yourself when you accomplish your goal with a trip to the local craft store to splurge on a new product you've been eyeing or with another reward of your choice.

Maintain a designated work space. Strive to keep your workstation organized and your most commonly used tools and supplies handy. Come to and leave a clean, at-ready work space to save invaluable time otherwise spent searching for items and getting situated. Additionally, keep an inventory of your product and replenish regularly to avoid coming to a standstill in the midst of inspired scrapbooking.

Organize as you go. Promptly develop film after finishing the roll and categorize all prints and negatives to keep from easily becoming inundated. Similarly, create page kits containing presorted product, photos and page sketches for efficient scrapbooking.

Prioritize projects. If you have a great deal to catch up on, or are a new scrapbooker unsure of where to begin, avoid becoming overwhelmed and discouraged by scrapbooking your most current photos first. In working backward in time, you record memories while they are fresh and keep incoming photos under control. Sort and scrapbook older photos and memorabilia once you feel you have a grasp on current projects.

Design quick and easy themed albums. Repeat techniques, colors, embellishments and composition styles in themed albums so as not to be faced with the task of designing a new masterpiece with each and every page. Save your most complicated and time-consuming pages for your favorite photos and document everyday others more simply.

Use the buddy system. Scrapbook with friends at home crops or through in-store workshops for creative motiva-tion and to put crafting time to dual use. By putting a social twist on scrapbooking, you can catch up with friends and produce pages all at the same time.

Make it a family affair. If you have young children at home, set up a small table or desk where they can create their own masterpieces alongside you while you scrapbook.

View scrapbooking time as your time. Turn on your favorite music, snack on a favorite treat and create an atmosphere where archiving your memories is a special and savored experience you'll look forward to engaging in again and again.

Idea inspiration for grown-up scrapbook pages

Coming to the craft table with a ready reserve of ideas is half the battle every scrapbooker faces. In the whirlwind that is adult life, it can be a challenge to channel those all-too-perfect ideas in a pinch. Look to these helpful page concepts when the time comes to chronicle glimpses into grown-up life and times.

Self-Inspired Layouts:

Little-known facts
A day in the life
Favorite and least favorite things
Life to-do list
Milestones and achievements
Beliefs and personal faith
Best advice ever received
Greatest accomplishments
Dreams and aspirations
Multifaceted roles
Strengths and weaknesses
Then-and-now self-assessment
Astrological sign and characteristics
Events of the year of your birth
Defining moments and decisions
Goals for self-improvement

Romance-Inspired Layouts:

The story of how you met
First impressions
When you knew you were in love
What told you he/she was "the one"
Top reasons you love one another
Anniversaries and highlights
What makes your relationship work
Favorite things to do together
Places that hold special significance
What strengthens your relationship
Individual and mutual hopes and dreams
The "little things" you do to show your love
Special songs and tokens of affection
Silliest pet peeves and areas of conflict
Challenges overcome
Recipe for a lasting relationship

Family-Inspired Layouts:

Memories of growing up
Instilled family values
Characteristics that run in the family
What makes a family
Most memorable occasions
Legendary family stories
Unique heritage and ancestry
Roles culture and religion play
Tributes to favorite relatives
Hardships encountered
Significant milestones
Valued heirlooms
Special recipes
Unique family traditions
Regular family rituals
Bits of wisdom for future generations

Friendship-Inspired Layouts:

How you came to be friends
Your most treasured friend
Why your friendship works
Qualities you admire most in your friend
How friends would describe you
Common interests
Biggest differences
Shared experiences
What your friendships have taught you
Unique ways various friends add to your life
Special acts of friendship
Definition of companionship
Ritual get-togethers and getaways
Favored ways of keeping in touch
Greatest moments shared
Pet pals

Recreation-Inspired Layouts:

Favorite hobbies and pastimes
Ways you express your creativity
Greatest passions
Most wild adventure
Major projects
Things you love most about your home
Home and garden maintenance
Around-the-house happenings
Prized possessions
Favorite ways to relax
Reasons you scrapbook
Top-ten ways to have fun
Favorite forms of entertainment
Ways you pamper yourself
Ideal ways to spend your alone time
Memorable travels

Vocation-Inspired Layouts:

What you wanted to be growing up
How your career goals have changed
Reasons you chose your particular career
How your current job came to be
On-the-job obstacles and challenges
First job, worst jobs and best-loved jobs
Favorite aspects about your work
Most influential mentors
Awards and recognition
Ambitions for the future
Favorite fellow employees
A typical workday
Your office and work space
Components of your dream job
Homemaking rewards and challenges
Transitioning from full-time to retirement

Tools and supplies

The rich smell of paint. A freshly sharpened colored pencil. The texture of paper. Crisp-cutting scissors. Many scrapbook supplies are craft staples we remember fondly from our earliest art experiences. Modern scrapbooking arsenals still call on the fundamentals for even the most cutting-edge creations. Only now these familiar tools and supplies represent more evolved, sophisticated successors intended for scrapbook art. Select supplies that spur your imagination and reflect your own ever-evolving style. In doing so you distinguish grown-up pages with a look all their own and give your adult years the spotlight they so deserve in scrapbooks.

Albums

Baby albums, school albums, wedding and travel albums—so many special aspects of life are honored with equally special and distinctive albums. While you may wish to incorporate adulthood pages into pre-existing albums, setting aside an album exclusively for your adult years gives them added emphasis. Numerous three-ring, post-bound and strap-hinge albums exist in various colors, sizes and themes perfect for your personality and the purpose you have for your pages.

Paper

This supplies staple has come a long way since the colored construction paper of our youth. Scrapbookers can choose from a rainbow of colors, textures, prints and specialty papers representing every shade of the imagination. For versatile backgrounds, accents and photo mats, incorporate coordinating patterns and themed papers to lend additional artistic flare perfect for grown-up pages. Use only acid- and lignin-free papers to protect your photos and memorabilia to ensure your albums have an extra-long shelf life.

Photos and memorabilia

Constantly maintain the mentality of a scrapbooker and dedicate yourself to documenting your adult accomplishments, special events and milestones with the fervor and foresight you would your children's. Additionally, collect mementos for keepsakes and record with your camera occasions you wish to remember in your scrapbook pages. To showcase your adult years center-stage, select those photos that feature you and favorite fellow grown-ups enjoying different aspects of adult life.

Templates and stencils

The laborious task of freehand drawing and cutting patterns has been alleviated with an astonishing array of templates and sten-cils. Encompassing innumerable shapes and themes, time-consuming steps are saved using these tools to crop photos, trace perfect figures and to create photo mats and die cuts. Bypass additional tedium by utilizing stencils that come with corresponding cutting tools for an all-in-one, precise finishing touch for achieving perfect shapes.

Adhesives

Craft adhesives have evolved from nostalgic standby staples such as Elmer's glue and rubber cement. In the time we've grown up, countless acid-free, photo-safe adhesives have been developed to keep our photos and keepsakes anchored to our pages in an archivally sound fashion. Glues, tapes and mounting corners of various sorts are essential supplies in every adult scrapbooking arsenal.

Colorants

Coloring inside the lines has never been so much fun thanks to the array of colorants now at your fingertips. You can relive your childhood love of coloring even though you're all grown up with chalks, paints, inks, tinted glues, colored pencils, embossing powders and pens and markers of every fathomable hue equivocal to the very best crayon collection. Show off your eye for sophisticated color schemes using acid-free colorants for vibrant, eye-catching pages.

Cutting tools

Remember the days when your mother's pinking shears were considered a striking, stand-out craft supply? They have been surpassed by a plethora of cutting tools that easily dress up photo mats and page accents. Additionally, the old guillotine-style paper cutters from your school days have graduated into compact, safe and easy-to-use paper trimmers with interchangeable patterned blades. Craft knives and countless punches provide for favorite cutting tools ideal for any design. Keeping your pages crisp and your edges clean has never been so simple with such cutting-edge cutting tools.

Design additions and embellishments

Relive the fun you remember from adolescence designing masterpieces with stamps, stickers and such, but this time in stylish, grown-up scrapbook pages. An array of just-the-right accents exists for every creative concept imaginable. Include die cuts, punches, brads, eyelets, metals, beads, baubles, organics and other artful "extras" to add instant pizazz to your pages. Strive to experiment with chic embellishments that signify how your grown-up style has evolved.

Chapter One

This Is Me □

Have you ever had the feeling that there was something missing from your scrapbooks? The next time you are admiring the fruits of your labor represented in well-placed embellishments and meticulously executed compositions, take stock to see how many of those spreads showcase the certain someone who created them. You. While many artists prefer to craft masterpieces inspired by outside muses, even the likes of Van Gogh left behind a sampling of precious self-portraits. Creating scrapbook pages that pay tribute to the artist behind the artistry are priceless interpretations of a one-of-a-kind life, personality and spirit. On these canvases of self-expression, you may convey your personal perspectives, reflections, accomplishments and dreams for the future. Perhaps most importantly, in documenting the experiences and insights that are completely, uniquely you, a lasting legacy is left in your scrapbooks for generations to appreciate. Now is the time to leave your artist's mark on all-about-you, self-celebration scrapbook pages.

Then And Now

Capture the past and present on a single page

Record and reflect on how your life has evolved with journaling and "then and now" photos. Start with a patterned paper background. Print "then" and "now" lists on blue cardstock; stamp edges with texture stamp in brown ink and adhere to page. Layer with patterned papers. For first part of title, age tag and calendar accent with walnut ink; stamp "THEN" onto calendar with letter stamps. Adhere both to upper left corner; adorn with gold spiral. Adhere photos over patterned papers. For second part of title, affix hand and letter stickers to brown cardstock square; mount on striped tag embellished with gold circle charm. To create collage tag accent, treat small tag with brown ink; stamp with postage stamp and adorn with green ribbon, stickers and clock face. Tie off with inked jute and mount on right corner of page.

Ann-Marie Weis, Oakland, California

Supplies: Patterned papers (Anna Griffin, Design Originals); texture stamp (All Night Media); gold spiral (7 Gypsies); letter stamps (Hero Arts); postage stamp (Stampington); striped tag (Foofala); letter, hand and collage stickers (EK Success); clock charm (www.scrapsahoy.com); blue and brown cardstocks; pocket calendar; small tag; walnut ink; gold circle charm; green ribbon; clock face

LauraLinda

Feature journaling and photo tags

Feature the most important aspects of your multi-faceted life with journaling and photo tags. Begin with preprinted background paper. Mat focal photo on brown cardstock. Tear vellum and color with gold metallic rub-ons; mount matted photo atop vellum. Print journaling on tan cardstock; tear out, crumple, flatten and enhance with metallic rub-ons. Mount matted photo onto journaling box. Set eyelets along bottom and right upper corner of journaling box. Mat smaller photos on brown cardstock. Tear bottoms from tags; mount photos. Set eyelets in tags and hang from journaling box with hemp cord. Print first part of title on tan cardstock; cut out, mat on brown cardstock and adhere with brads. Cut second part of title from vellum treated with gold metallic rub-ons using craft knife and lettering template. Double mat first letters on brown cardstock and clear vellum; adhere to page. Set eyelet above "i" in title.

LauraLinda Rudy, Markham, Ontario, Canada

Supplies: Preprinted background paper (Cloud 9 Design); metallic rub-ons (Craf-T); lettering templates (Scrap Pagerz); tan and brown cardstocks; vellum; brads; eyelets; hemp cord

Virgo

What's your sign?

Give your layout a celestial zing with a page dedicated to your astrological sign. Begin with a textured blue cardstock background. Adhere section from gray paper vertically to right side of page. Affix strip of vellum to top of page; accent with thin strip of gray cardstock and brad. Tear section from brown cardstock and adhere vertically along left side of page. Cut top from "Virgo" patterned paper and adhere to top of page; add faux wax seal. For journaling block, print astrological characteristics onto vellum; cut out and mount with gray cardstock strip and brad. Layer various strips of gray, blue and tan cardstocks to form layered border strips for side and bottom of page; accent with brads. Create accents by double matting Zodiac cut-outs on gray and blue cardstocks; adhere journaling strips with brads to torn cardstock border strip. Mat photo on tan cardstock; affix to page at an angle, tucking partially under title border and Zodiac accent.

Jami Myers, Apache Junction, Arizona

Supplies: Textured blue & brown cardstocks (Bazzill); Virgo patterned paper, zodiac cut-outs (Carolee's Creations); faux wax seal (Creative Imaginations); tan cardstock; vellum; brads

When I Was Born

Journal about the year of your birth

Go photoless on your next layout to keep an interesting journaling passage the primary focus. Begin with denim background paper. Tear sections from patterned paper; treat with sienna ink and adhere to page at right side and corners. Print journaling on cream cardstock; trim and smudge with sienna ink. Set copper eyelets at beginning of each sentence; adhere to background. Ink scrap burlap lightly in sienna; mount above journaling. Cut year from patterned paper using craft knife and template; adhere along with letter stickers for title. Use brown photo mat for journaling frame; embellish with nostalgic stickers, label, rub-on word, button, torn sections of inked patterned paper and metal washer word. Embellish bottom page corner with coin holder, calendar and clock face embellishment. Slide metal ribbon charm onto inked cream ribbon and attach to page.

Tarri Botwinski, Grand Rapids, Michigan

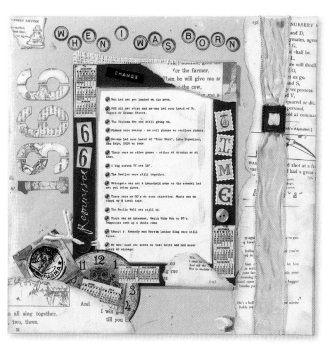

Supplies: Patterned papers (Rusty Pickle); letters, stamp, time, and calendar stickers (Creative Imaginations); template (source unknown); metal washer word, rub-on words, ribbon charm (Making Memories); coin holder (2DYE4); cream cardstock; sienna ink; copper eyelets; brown photo mat; label maker

Supplies: Patterned paper, poem stone, letter stickers, faux wax seal (Creative Imaginations); spiral clip (Making Memories); conchos (Scrapworks); vellum; tan, and rose cardstocks; fiber; brown chalk, wheat floss

Time, Time, Time...

Create a "self-centered" collage

A collage-style spread is a great way to showcase several photos and paper techniques. Begin with two wine-colored cardstock background pages. For left page, start by tearing bottom edge and top right corner from patterned paper; adhere to page. Layer with additional piece of patterned paper torn in the same fashion; affix over top of background page and adhere in back to create a flap. Add punched circle accent adorned with concho and fibers. Create photo tag from patterned paper; embellish with concho and fiber. Tuck into patterned papers. Affix focal photo to center layer. Layer bottom of page with torn patterned papers. Glue bottom and right edges to background to create pocket for vellum journaling tag. Layer with transparency strip and torn patterned paper. Create a flap by adhering to page along left side only with conchos. Embellish with small photo, caption and swirl clip. Print journaling for small photo onto cardstock; tear out, chalk edges and adhere to left side of patterned paper pocket. Add "pull" and "lift" tabs to vellum tag and transparency flap. Create title with sticker letters. For right page, vertically layer torn sections from patterned papers; attach with conchos to form pockets. Adhere photos. Hang tag from concho; adorn with poem stone. Print journaling onto vellum; cut into tag shape and strip for photo. Slide vellum tag into patterned paper layer; add "pull" tab. Mount caption from patterned paper and envelope to page. Print saying onto transparency; cut out and adhere along with torn wine cardstock strip, faux wax seal and small jewelry tag.

Sandy Brantley, Jacksonville, Florida

Things I Love

Say it with journaling strips

Summarize that which you love most with journaling strips and meaningful photos. Begin with textured rose-colored cardstock background. Cut section from patterned paper; tear top and bottom edge. Layer with cut section from pink patterned paper. Use letter stamps and pink ink to apply title to tan paper; cut into strip and adhere over top of torn paper. Mat photos on rose-colored cardstock; adhere to page. Print the things you love on strips of tan cardstock treated with pink ink; affix randomly across page. Alter edges of manila tag with pink ink; layer with pink patterned paper, white costal netting and photo of flower. Tie off tag with fibers and adhere on bottom right corner of page.

Nicole LaCour, Memory Makers magazine

Supplies: Textured rose-colored cardstock (Bazzill); patterned papers (Creative Imaginations); white coastal netting (Magic Scraps); letter stamps (Prickley Pear); tan cardstock; manila tag; fibers

How Will I
Remember
This Moment?

Record introspective thoughts

Use self-portraits and reflective journaling to muse on where you are at this point in your life. Begin by layering two ivory cardstock backgrounds with gray and blue cardstocks and pre-printed transparency circles, strips, and squares; chalk edges of cardstock squares in brown. For the left page, mat photo on tan cardstock and adhere. Print part of title on tan cardstock; cover "i" in dimensional adhesive. Cut circle opening from transparency; layer over title. Stamp and cut remainder of title using envelope for stamping and lettering template for tan cardstock letters. Tear edges from envelope; accent with dimensional adhesive and sprinkle with tiny glass marbles. Adhere to page; insert extra photos. Chalk cardstock letters; adhere "m" on tan cardstock embellished with glass marbles; affix on page. Embellish transparency with stamped compass that has been cut out; mount with watch crystal to create shaker filled with tiny beads. On right page, alter photo using Microsoft Picture It!; double mat on gray and tan cardstocks and adhere on page. Affix remaining photos. Print journaling on transparency; cut out and mount on page. Embellish page with tan square cardstock covered with tiny glass beads.

Jody Sorey, Prairieville, Louisiana

Supplies: Preprinted transparencies, beads (Magic Scraps); dimensional adhesive (Plaid); letter stamps (PSX Design); compass stamp (Hero Arts); lettering template (Provo Craft); watch crystal (Scrapworks); ivory, tan, blue and gray cardstocks; transparency; small envelope; brown chalk

Winter Out West

Feature organic page elements

Bring a little of the "wild" into a western layout by incorporating feathers for an outdoorsy feel. Begin with a brown cardstock background. Braid embroidery floss into four ropes long enough to go end to end vertically on page; mount in two sections 1½" apart along right side of page. Punch five 2" squares from various suede papers and five from cardstock. Adhere feathers to cardstock with spray adhesive; trim off excess. Mount all squares atop braided ropes, alternating suede and feather squares. Affix western-themed dimensional stickers. Double mat photo on tan and brown suede papers; accent with hand-sewn "X"s. Journal on tan cardstock and mat on suede paper. Tear corner strips from vellum; sew onto journaling using "X" pattern. Cut title from tan cardstock using lettering template and craft knife; layer on page with feather. Complete title by printing on vellum; tear and affix over first part of title.

Alissa Jones, San Diego, California
Photo: Marie Beschen, Escondido, California

Supplies: Textured brown cardstock, suede papers (Bazzill); feathers (Darice); vellum; lettering template (Accu-Cut); dimensional stickers (EK Success); wheat embroidery floss

To-Do List

Scrapbook your goals

Take an extra step in committing yourself to conquering your life to-do list by incorporating it into a layout for others to see. Begin with a brown textured cardstock background. Tear sections of pink textured cardstock and patterned paper; treat edges with dark pink ink. Layer torn sections to form border; attach together with torn strips of brown crumpled paper set with eyelets. String and tie hemp cord through eyelets; adhere border to page. Layer photo on page along with torn textured pink cardstock; treat with ink. Tear and crumple strip of brown paper; embellish with eyelets and hemp and mount atop photo. Stamp date on cardstock. Print to-do list on white vellum; cut out and tear off bottom edge. Print quote on ivory vellum; tear out, stamp on date and layer with to-do list on page with brads.

Michaela Young-Mitchell, Morenci, Arizona
Photo: Ronda Samuelson, Clifton, Arizona

Supplies: Textured brown and pink cardstocks (Bazzill); patterned paper (7 Gypsies); date stamp (Staples); brown paper; eyelets; brads; hemp cord; dark pink ink

The Key To Being Kent

Pick the perfect page adornments

Play off words in your title with just the right page embellishments. Begin with coordinating patterned papers for background pages. For left page, cut out preprinted keys; adhere to left side of page. Mat photo on vellum and attach to page with gold brads; adorn with key cut-out. Print title onto vellum; cut out and mount with brads atop key cut-out embellishment. For right page, enlarge and print original photo onto vellum; cut out and mount with spray adhesive. Add additional key cut-outs atop photo. Print journaling onto vellum; layer at skewed angle over vellum-printed photo, attaching with brads.

Ginger McSwain, Cary, North Carolina

Supplies: Patterned papers (SEI); key cut-outs (EK Success); vellum; gold brads

Twenty-One

Remember each year with a letter

Make writing a letter to yourself a yearly goal to record a snapshot-in-time glimpse on a scrapbook page. Begin with a dark blue cardstock background. Crumple cream cardstock, flatten, cut off top section and tear off bottom section; ink torn edge and mount on page. Repeat with a smaller section of brown patterned paper; stamp image of streets of Paris onto paper. Enlarge photo and add text using Adobe Photoshop 7.0. Journal letter to yourself on cream cardstock; cut out and treat edges with black ink. Adhere journaling, photo and cut sections of flower photo paper on page. Cut tag from flower photo paper; use letter stamp to apply initial. Thread cut strip of blue cardstock through tag; mount along with flower appliqué on page.

Rebecca Cantu, Brownwood, Texas

Supplies: Paris stamp, letter stamp (Hero Arts); flower photo paper (Cropper Hopper); letter stamp (Hero Arts); flower appliqué (Wal-Mart); blue and cream cardstocks; black ink

Focusing On Me

Supplies: Gold leafing pen (Krylon); photo hangers (Victoria Art Supply); gold letter stickers (Pioneer); page pebble (Making Memories); orange and brown cardstocks; brown eyelets; orange ribbon; gold metallic paper; copper brads

Mimic a camera lens with circles

Incorporate bold circle embellishments and clean lines for a picture-perfect layout. Begin with two dark orange cardstock backgrounds. Print title and journaling directly onto background pages. Cut several cardstock circles and strips; edge some of the circles with gold foil pen. Adhere strips and circles throughout pages, forming borders with layered strips; accent with eyelets. Attach to pages, making sure to align cardstock border strips and sectioned circle when pages are placed together. Wrap and secure orange ribbon vertically around left page. Mat focal photo on brown cardstock edged with gold foil pen. Affix to left page. Mat square-punched photos on orange cardstock squares that have been edged with foil pen. Adhere photo hangers on back of orange mats. Mat again on brown cardstock squares edged in gold pen. Hang matted photos to each other with ribbon; glue matted photos to left page to secure. To finish right page, mat "me" onto orange cardstock; cut out and mat on gold-edged brown cardstock and attach to border strip with copper brads. Use gold letter stickers for date; cover with page pebble. Mat photo on gold-edged brown cardstock mat; adhere to page. Affix cut circle atop photo.

Sharon Whitehead, Vernon, British Columbia, Canada

Beauty Of A Woman

Hold that thought in a vellum envelope

Privately preserve a personal reflection by tucking it inside an envelope within your layout. Begin with an orange cardstock background page. Enlarge photo; cut out and mount on background. Print title and poem on copper cardstock; age slightly with chestnut ink. Tear out, ink torn edges and adhere both sections to page. Apply stickers. Affix vellum envelope to copper cardstock square; add stickers on each side, tear out, ink torn edges and mount on page. Journal thought onto cardstock; crop and slip inside envelope for safekeeping.

Kim Musgrove, Lewiston, New York

Supplies: Textured orange cardstock (Bazzill); stickers (Magenta); vellum envelope (EK Success); copper cardstock; chestnut ink

Turning Point

Seek solace in a scrapbook page

Recording and reflecting upon the trials and triumphs of dealing with an illness can be therapeutic when expressed within the pages of a scrapbook. For left page, mount focal photo on brown cardstock background. Layer with cut-outs and frame that have been altered by sanding, tearing and chalking. Tear orange cardstock strip for border; chalk in burgundy and adhere to page with small photo. Print journaling onto yellow vellum and heat set with clear embossing powder; tear out, chalk torn edges in burgundy and mount. Affix title beneath focal photo with brads. For right page, adhere photo to orange cardstock background. Journal above directly onto page. Add date stamp and layer with altered cut-out frame; accent with stamped tag. Tear and alter cut-out accent; adhere beside photo. Print journaling onto orange paper; tear sides, chalk and layer over center of page. Emboss yellow vellum; tear, chalk and mount on page, layering some beneath altered cut-outs.

Sue Kelemen, St. Louis, Missouri

Supplies: Cut-out collage element paper (Cloud 9 Design); date stamp (Making Memories); orange and brown cardstocks; vellum; embossing powder; spiral clip; chalk; antique brads; small tag

I Am Beautiful

Celebrate your self-acceptance

Use envelopes containing facts and figures about the average woman to show your acceptance and pride in who *you* are. Begin with two olive-colored cardstock backgrounds. Print part of title directly onto left background page. Print remaining title on olive cardstock; cut out letters at angles and treat with brown and orange inks; mount with foam adhesive. Cut and tear sections from orange cardstock for both background pages; adhere. On left page, mount enlarged photo. Create seal by squeezing orange faux wax from a hot glue gun onto small inked cardstock square. While warm, stamp with Chinese image; adhere to bottom of page. For right page, cut tops from manila envelopes and treat with olive ink. Embellish each envelope as desired using charms, ribbons, photos, heart-stamped wax seals, papers and page pebbles; mount on page. Print facts and figures on cardstock tags; tie off with leather lacing and slip into envelopes.

Emily Garza, Layton, Utah

Supplies: Faux wax (www.scrapsahoy.com); page pebbles (Making Memories); olive and orange cardstocks; brown and orange inks; ribbon; envelopes; leather strips; fiber; charms

About Me At Age 33

House journaling tags inside sewn pockets

What would your husband want your kids to know years from now about him today? Have him write it onto tags for an informative layout. Begin with a red faux-textured background page. For pocket border, cut section from tan cardstock. Glue hemp cords on back side of cardstock where the edges of each pocket will be. Flip over and emboss along both sides of cord with bone folder; machine sew pockets onto background. Adhere torn sections from striped patterned paper to each pocket. Cut strip from tan cardstock; emboss using pattern plate and adhere to top of pockets. Stamp questions with various letter stamps on white cardstock. Cut out title and tear out questions; age by crumpling and chalking in brown. Attach questions to pockets with button, swirl clip, antique brad and tiny eyelets. For title block, stamp first and last portions of title on white cardstock; crumple and chalk in brown. Create mat by tearing right and bottom edges from brown cardstock; chalk edges in brown. Stamp remainder of title on brown cardstock; adhere frame and mount on title box. Triple mat photo on white cardstock, tan cardstock and brown cardstock; mount on page. For journaling tags, cut from brown cardstock; set two eyelets at top and string brown beads through with jute.

Jennifer Lessinger, Rockville, Minnesota

Supplies: Patterned papers (Daisy D's, K & Company); pattern plate (Fiskars); letter stamps (Hero Arts, PSX Design); antique snaps, silver frame (Making Memories); tan, brown and white cardstocks; eyelets; beads; button; swirl clip; tiny eyelets; hemp cord; brown chalk; black ink

A Dream Lives Forever

Document your dreams

Create a customized envelope to be the keeper of your dreams on a page about determination. Begin with a patterned paper background. Print photo with white border; mat on burgundy paper, leaving extra length at bottom. Tear off bottom of mat; tear edge from torn piece. Wrap photo with fiber; tie on tag that has been aged with walnut ink. Journal "believe" on tag. Adhere photo along with torn strip to page. Embellish strip with burgundy buttons. Affix section of copper mesh on page. Create envelope from burgundy paper; set burgundy eyelets in brown cardstock squares and mount on flaps. Journal inside, fold and secure with wheat embroidery floss. Adhere over mesh onto page.

Rhonda Palmer, Pittsburg, Kansas

Supplies: Patterned paper (Creative Imaginations); copper mesh (Magic Mesh); walnut ink; brown cardstock; burgundy paper; fiber; small tag; burgundy buttons; burgundy eyelets; wheat embroidery floss

My Backpack & Me

Feature a favorite personal item

Create a telling layout by documenting what a particular treasured possession says about you. Start with light green cardstock background pages. For left page, print journaling onto lime-colored cardstock; mat on background. Tear strip of patterned vellum and adhere to top of page. Double mat photo on purple cardstocks, leaving space for part of title; adhere. Treat letter cut-outs with olive-colored ink; adhere over punch-out circle frame and photo mat. Layer bottom of page with strip of embossed purple paper and green ribbon. For right page, layer lime-colored cardstock, strip of embossed purple paper and section of purple paper on background page. Print journaling on light purple cardstock; cut out and adhere. Print portion of page title on green patterned paper; cut into strip and adhere across page. Mat photo on purple cardstock and mount. Tear patterned vellum and layer over top left side of page. Adhere punch-out frame and inked cut-out letters with foam adhesive to square cut-out frame. Create remainder of title with cut-out letters mounted over cut-out circle frame.

Ann-Marie Weis, Oakland, California

Yellow cell phone
3 kinds of lip gloss
Sunscreen stick
Handspring Visor PDA
2 kinds of moisturizers
Mini first aid kit
2 pens
Tylenol
2 small kids' travel games
2 used Kleenexes
Wallet stuffed with receipts
Maxalt migraine pills
Old grocery list
3 pennies
2 half eaten potato chips bags
Photocopies of our passports and social
security cards
Small container with Aspirin
Old crumbs

Supplies: Patterned vellum (source unknown); patterned papers (Anna Griffin); punch-out frames and patterned papers (Chatterbox); cut-out letters (Foofala); purple embossed cardstock (source unknown); lime green cardstock; light green cardstock, light and dark purple cardstocks; purple paper; olive ink; green ribbon

. . . *what it says about*

I am a very practical person
I like to hold my kids' hands
I believe in having backup options
I love travel sizes
I have very dry hands
I am highly organized, but messy
I married a man with bad headaches
I do not clean out my backpack very often
I am prepared for accidents, pain, impatience, hunger, and random controls by the INS
There is more to me than meets the eye

My Favorites

Document what you enjoy most

Share a few of your favorite things in an all-about-you page. Begin with a black cardstock background. Enlarge a photo to create blurred effect; cut out section and mount on upper left side of page. Print your name and a sampling of your favorite things in various fonts onto transparency. Cut name into strip and mount over photo scrap from enlargement; adhere to top of page. Affix transparency over blurred photo image. Add stick pin to bottom of transparency. Print enlarged black-and-white photo with white border; triple mat on yellow, pink and lime cardstocks. Adhere fibers to bottom of photo; mount on page. Cut images and sentiment from greeting card; mount on bottom of page. String silver rings onto ribbon and mount across bottom of page. Adhere magnetic poetry words to ribbon to finish.

Martha Crowther, Salem, New Hampshire

Supplies: Rings (7 Gypsies); textured lime cardstock (Bazzill); magnetic poetry words (Magnetic Poetry); stick pin; transparency; black, yellow and pink cardstocks; fibers

Finding Joy In Myself

Reflect on what makes you happy

Journaling all of your deepest feelings can bring an acceptance of things with which you have struggled. Begin with a striped patterned paper background page. Layer center of page with torn patterned vellum and purple paper strips. Double mat photo on purple patterned paper and coordinating striped patterned paper; fold corners of striped mat over corners of photo and adhere on page over torn vellum strip. Add clear self-adhesive frame over portion of photo. Create title by applying various letter stickers to patterned paper. Affix tag with brad onto torn vellum strip. Mount clear self-adhesive circle frame over tag. Tie purple ribbon to clear self-adhesive tag and apply over first part of title. To create pocket, cut large square from green patterned paper; tear off left edge and adhere top, right and bottom edges. Adorn with strips of paper and journaled words. Create tag for pocket from patterned paper; journal and accent with purple rivet and ribbon. Slip tag into pocket.

Anna Armendariz, McChord Air Force Base, Washington
Photo: Alexander Lommel, Anchorage, Alaska

Supplies: Patterned papers, vellum, letter stickers, "joy" tag, purple rivet (Chatterbox); clear self-adhesive frames and tag (K & Company); purple ribbon; brad

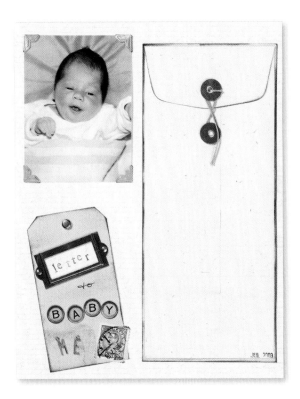

Letter To Baby Me

Reflect on life in a letter to yourself

Creating a layout that includes a letter to yourself as a baby is a great way to muse on where life has taken you. Adhere photo to patterned paper background page with gold photo corners. Write letter and insert into tall envelope. Create mat for envelope from natural-colored cardstock; ink edges in black. Adhere matted envelope onto page. Treat envelope by lightly smearing ink pad across tag surface and edges; adhere on page with gold brad. For tag accent, ink in same technique as envelope. Stamp part of title on patterned paper, cut out and affix under label holder; adhere to tag. Complete title with your own handwriting, letter stickers and metal letter charms; embellish with stamp sticker. Stamp date of letter on bottom corner of envelope to finish.

Amanda Goodwin, Munroe Falls, Ohio

Supplies: patterned paper (7 Gypsies); gold photo corners (Canson); envelope, bookplate (www.twopeasinabucket.com); letter stamps (PSX Design); letter and stamp stickers (EK Success); date stamp (Making Memories); gold brad; metal letter charms

Parts And Pieces Of Me

Create a flip-style journal

Give your loved ones a glimpse into your heart with a small journal containing all of your blessings, passions and loves. Print title and quote directly onto white cardstock and mat on black cardstock background. Mount focal photo on black cardstock; adhere at top left corner. Crop sections from extra photos and adhere to page. Journal inside small notebook. Alter cover by layering patterned transparency, punched red heart and white cardstock. Adhere printed "lift" strip wrapped around edge of notebook cover. Finish page by adhering metal date plate on bottom left corner.

Joanna Bolick, Fletcher, North Carolina

Supplies: Small notebook (Global Solutions); transparency (Magic Scraps); black metal date plate (EK Success); black, white and red cardstocks

One Defining Moment

Reflect upon a turning point with journaling

Use meaningful quotes to help express how you emerged from a tumultuous time. Begin with a brown patterned paper background. Create top border by layering strips of brown and green patterned papers. Tie jute around left side of border, leaving lengths to "hang" quotes and journaling block. Print title on white paper; tear out, crumple, roll torn edges and adhere over border. Double mat photo on brown cardstock and green patterned paper. Create photo frame from green cardstock. Tear and roll edges; affix atop photo. Adorn frame with cork circles and knotted jute cord. Dangle additional cork circles from jute; braid and knot together at top. Glue knot to torn green square and affix to border. Print quotes and journaling on white paper; tear out and mat on cork sheets and torn green and tan papers. Adhere over jute cords to page.

Lori McClain, Yorktown, Indiana
Photo: Bruce McClain, Yorktown, Indiana

Supplies: Patterned paper (Provo Craft); cork sheets, cork shapes (Scrappin' Safari); brown, white and green papers; jute

Getting To Know The Real Jason

Create tiny photo boxes

Interview a sibling and feature the facts and other findings you uncover with small photo boxes and bullet-style journaling. Begin with a textured orange cardstock background. Print focal photo with white border; adhere on background. Use a word-processing program to form 1 x 1" text boxes. Scan in photos and paste them into the text boxes; print. Journal in bullet-style format on textured green cardstock. Cut out and mat on textured black cardstock; add tiny photos and mount on page around focal photo. Apply title on bottom of background with rub-on letters.

Janetta Abucejo Wieneke, Memory Makers Books

Supplies: Textured cardstocks (Bazzill); rub-on letters (Creative Imaginations)

Daryl

Custom design a digital frame

Use a photo-editing software program to create a patriotic backdrop for your page. Begin with a black cardstock background. Create digital frame by opening new document in Adobe Photoshop 7.0; color background black. Select text tool and add title; go into layers and add a drop shadow. Add remaining text to bottom of background using white, red, blue and yellow text. Print onto photo paper, cut out and adhere to black cardstock background. Cut section from holographic paper and mat on white cardstock; adhere to center of digital background. Punch squares from photos and mount diagonally down digital background with foam adhesive. Finish by adding dimensional star stickers to top and bottom of page.

MaryJo Regier, Memory Makers Books

Supplies: Holographic paper (Weekend Cropper); dimensional star stickers (Hirschberg Schutz & Co.); black and white cardstocks

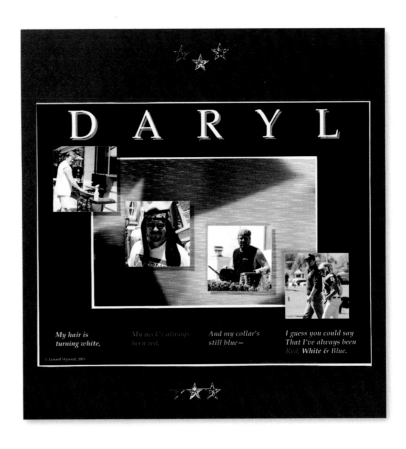

Supplies: White corrugated paper (DMD); label maker (Dymo); triangle tag (7 Gypsies); jewels (Westrim); black cardstock; gold fiber; gold eyelets; gold Scorpio charm

MJ-ology

Feature your little-known facts with labels

Create a tidy-looking collage by corralling it all inside a customized label frame. Begin with a black cardstock background. Adhere section of white corrugated paper to page. Use a label maker to craft labels for words and phrases that describe you; adhere along edges of white corrugated paper. Trim red cardstock and cut oval opening for photo frame. Alter photo in Adobe Photoshop 7.0, adding a neon-glow filter effect. Print and affix behind oval opening and adhere to corrugated mat. On a piece of cardstock, create a collage by gluing pieces of paper, photos, jewels and stamped words that describe you. Add a triangle tag with gold eyelets to upper right corner; slide printed quote or caption into tag. Tie Scorpio charm with gold fiber to tag. Trim collage to fit within red mat. Cut a slightly larger oval opening and mount on red frame.

MaryJo Regier, Memory Makers Books

All About Mrs. B

Fashion a book-style layout

Turn a two-page spread into a single layout by attaching the left page to the right with handmade hinges. Begin by tearing edges from black patterned paper; affix white cardstock strip to left edge. Create large tag from patterned paper matted on torn white cardstock; add conchos and fibers to ends. Embellish with beads, tiles, paper frame, paper circles and silver letter charms hung from beaded wire rings. Attach to first page. Adorn remainder of page with torn patterned papers, epoxy words, swirl clips, beads, paper frames and circles, tags and fibers. Adhere black-and-white photo to patterned paper; accent with black photo corners. For interior page, print journaling onto vellum and attach to patterned paper with white brads; mount on textured white cardstock and black and white striped background. To attach pages together, fashion hinges from patterned paper strips; attach to top, middle and bottom of first page along white cardstock strip with silver brads. Adhere strips to background of interior page.

Wendy Bickford, Antelope, California

Supplies: Patterned papers, paper frames and circles (KI Memories); white textured cardstock (Bazzill); epoxy words (Creative Imaginations); metal charm letters, swirl clips (Making Memories); tiles (Magic Scraps); silver and white brads; beads; silver charms; fibers

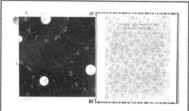

29

Celebrate your age

Dedicate a page to your perspective and accomplishments at a particular age. Journal directly onto kraft cardstock background. Layer strips of textured red cardstock, patterned paper and black mesh to form border along left side. Stamp age across textured red cardstock strip. Attach paper cut-out tag on red strip with black brads. Double mat photo on white and red cardstocks; treat edges with black ink. Leave extra length on the red cardstock mat; adhere onto page. Affix letter beads down edge of patterned paper border. Cut age from patterned paper using stencil; treat edges with black ink and adhere to page. Finish page by hanging metal numbers with black brad from photo mat.

Jennifer Bourgeault, Macomb Township, Michigan

Supplies: Textured red cardstock (Bazzill); patterned paper, cut-out tag, black brads (Chatterbox); black mesh (Magic Mesh); letter beads (Darice); number stamps (PSX Design); metal numbers (Making Memories); number stencil (Michaels); kraft cardstock; black ink

Chapter Two

the Power of

Way back when …
Two houses
Two cars
Two jobs
Two lives
Two hearts ready to love.

And now …
One home
One family
One card to find each Wednesday
One bowl of chips & hot sauce on Friday nights
One dozen roses just because
One dream come true
One love to last a lifetime.

This is the power of *One*

One

Love Stories □

It's the universal language and a song between two souls. It's the stuff of dreams and fairy tales and the sustenance of our spirits. Love has moved us through the ages to artistically profess the fortune of finding that special someone to share our lives with. Like valentines of sorts, love-themed scrapbook pages hearken back to an era where romantics created handmade tokens to display their affections. Crafting modern scrapbook pages provides a perfect and equally heartfelt forum to orchestrate Cupid's work. A budding new romance may be chronicled step by heart-palpitating step. The musings of a decades-long partnership may be revealed to inspire hope in the hearts of those still searching. Tender reflections on love's trials, tribulations and triumphs may be preserved for future porch swing recollections. First encounters. Mounting feelings. Inspired devotion. Resounding "I do's." When you find that true companion, immortalize the love you share in scrapbook pages that sustain those precious moments forever.

Supplies: *Patterned papers (Provo Craft); black handmade paper (Graphic Products); blended fibers texture gel, gray, silver and white acrylic paints (Liquitex); decorative photo corners (Hobby Lobby); woven labels (Me & My Big Ideas); silver hinge (Foofala); silver box closure (7 Gypsies); letter stickers, label holder, type keys, silver frames, embossed metal tile, heart charm (Nunn Design); watch crystal (Scrapworks); watch parts (Jest Charming); glass bottle (Card Connection); bead (Blue Moon Beads); love charm (source unknown); black cardstock; silver brads*

Romance

Incorporate acrylic paint

Alter a page background with acrylic paint for an added artistic touch. Begin by layering pieces of patterned papers and black handmade papers on page. Mix texture gel with silver, white and black acrylic paints; apply to page. Mat top and bottom photos on black handmade paper; adhere along with unmatted photo to page. Print journaling onto vellum; tear out and mount on page. Embellish photos with decorative corners, silver hinges and woven labels. Embellish page with letter stickers covered with silver type keys, silver frames, black embossed metal tile, heart charm, watch crystal shaker with beads and clock pieces, glass bottle filled with beads and accented with love charm and silver label holder attached over woven label with silver brads.

Carrie Zohn, Monroe, North Carolina

28 Reasons Why He Loves Me

Design personalized background paper

Create instant personalized patterned paper by printing the reasons he loves you onto cardstock. Begin with a black cardstock background. Use computer to repeat "reasons" until page is covered; print, trim, ink edges in black and mount on cardstock background. Double mat photo on patterned paper and pink cardstock treated with black ink; mat and adhere to page. Alter a small envelope with black ink and affix to page. Cut heart from pink patterned paper; ink edges in black and layer with torn pink mulberry. Crumple pink tag; flatten, ink edges in black and tie off with black ribbon. Apply title with letter stickers to tag and heart. Print "reasons" onto small piece of handmade paper; mat on black cardstock and insert along with tag into envelope. Adhere silver charm necklace across bottom of page. Stamp date at bottom left corner.

Candi Gershon, Fishers, Indiana

Supplies: *Textured black cardstock (Bazzill); pink tag (2DYE4); letter stickers (Me & My Big Ideas); silver charm necklace (found at local dollar store); date stamp (Making Memories); mulberry paper; black ink; black ribbon; small envelope*

Supplies: Black, green, red, blue and gray cardstocks

Our Colorful Marriage

Create color contrast with photos

Create an eye-catching layout by combining color and black-and-white photos. Begin with two black cardstock background pages. For left page, print journaling and part of title on gray cardstock; cut out title and affix across page. Cut remainder of title from green, red and blue cardstocks with craft knife using fonts as guides. Mat letters on green, red and blue cardstock squares and adhere to title strip. Mount journaling block on page. Mat bottom photo on gray cardstock; adhere along with remaining photos to page. For right page, double mat one photo at askew angle on gray and red cardstocks, leaving space at left edge for journaling. Print a caption repeatedly in different fonts on green, red and blue cardstocks; adhere to mat. Mat remaining photos on green, red and blue cardstocks and adhere to page.

Janelle Clark, Yorktown, Virginia
Photos: Caroline Davis, Mentor, Ohio

You Really Know How To Turn Me On

Light up your layout with a switch plate

Who knew an accent acquired from the hardware store could be a perfect addition to a love-inspired layout? Begin with a black cardstock background. Ink rose and brown patterned papers in black; sand rose patterned paper. Layer on background page. Mount photos and accent with photo corners. Soak packing tape strip affixed to patterned paper in warm water until paper begins to disintegrate. Rub paper off. Strip will be somewhat tacky; adhere along bottom of page. Mount cut-out letters for title on brown paper. Apply rub-on word to photo. Tie heart charm to red fibers and down center of layout. Stamp "Valentine" onto tag and dangle from fibers. Print journaling on manila cardstock; cut out, ink edges in black and layer over mica. Print "ON" onto manila cardstock scrap and adhere to back of light plate; mount on page to complete title. Cut ends off screws; glue heads to screw holes in plate. Stamp "over" onto bottom right side of page; adhere pointing finger cut-out below. Stamp date on bottom left side of page. Mount cards and additional mementos on back of layout.

Robin Hohenstern, Brooklyn Park, Minnesota

Supplies: Textured black cardstock (Bazzill); rose patterned paper (Hot Off The Press); brown patterned paper (Rusty Pickle); cut-out letters (Foofala); rub-on words (Making Memories); heart wine charm (Target); letter stamps (Hero Arts); pointing finger (EK Success); mica (USArtQuest); brown photo corners; packing tape; light switch plate; screws

Supplies: Textured black cardstock (Bazzill); mesh (Magic Mesh); patterned papers (7 Gypsies, KI Memories); letter stamps (Rubber Stampede); stitched tin, date stamp, page pebble (Making Memories); love charm (American Traditional); red and white cardstocks; black and red inks

Just Another Reason

Record a romantic surprise

Keep a romantic gesture forever fresh by preserving it with a striking photo. Begin with a white cardstock background. Treat edges of red cardstock and various patterned papers with black ink. Layer entire page along with sections from textured black cardstock and red mesh. Print and stamp "red roses" on white cardstock; cut into circle and treat edges with red ink. Mat on textured black cardstock. Layer enlarged photo over right half of page; slip circle partially underneath and adhere. Treat outer edges of photo with black ink. Journal on white cardstock; tear out, ink edges in black and mount across page. Adhere page pebble over "love." Attach silver love charm with silver brad to red cardstock circle that has been inked in black. Stitch circle tin with red floss; adhere love charm to stitched tin and mount on journaling strip. Stamp date on bottom of photo.

Jennifer Lessinger, Rockville, Minnesota

Marking

Mimic the look of handmade paper

You can create the look of handmade paper by using a technique with cardstock and water. Begin with two black cardstock background pages. Run moss-colored cardstock under water; crumple and flatten. Use hot iron to dry all but edges of cardstock. Roll edges with finger. Cut into strips and adhere to background pages. For left page, print journaling onto burgundy cardstock, leaving room at the left for matted photo. Mat photo on black cardstock and affix to burgundy cardstock. Crop secondary photos to fit square metal-rimmed vellum tags. Run photos through adhesive-application machine and affix to backs of vellum tags. Adhere tags to page with foam spacers. Hang with fiber from black brads affixed to center of page. For right page, apply rub-on word to metal rimmed rectangle tag; string black bead and hang from black brad. Mount six uniformly cropped photos on a burgundy cardstock mat. Affix matted photos to page to finish.

Kneka Smith, Phoenix, Arizona

Supplies: Metal-rimmed tags (Making Memories); word sticker (Bo-Bunny); black, moss and burgundy cardstocks; black brad; black bead

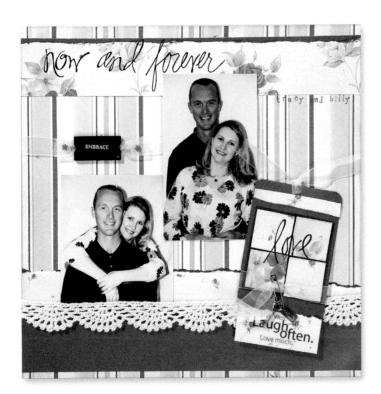

Supplies: Patterned paper, rub-on words (Making Memories); red flower tacks (Chatterbox); embrace label (Me & My Big Ideas); vellum quote (Memories Complete); silver charms (source unknown); lace trim; sheer ribbon; black label holder; black ink; black cardstock; safety pin; stamps

Now And Forever

Add texture with lace trim

Incorporating lace trim lends an easy romantic feel to a page inspired by love. Begin with a patterned paper background. Fashion borders by layering torn patterned paper and burgundy cardstock. Treat torn edges with black ink. Adhere lace trim to bottom border; affix borders to background. Stamp names below top border. Mount photos on page. Thread sheer yellow ribbon through sides of black label holder; affix "embrace" label underneath. Secure ends with red flower tacks. Adhere ribbon to page by adhering one end under photo and securing the other to back of page. Cut double tag from burgundy cardstock and flower patterned paper; tear off bottom of burgundy tag and ink torn edge. Punch four squares from patterned paper; mat on black cardstock and affix to tag. Apply rub-on words to squares and top border for title. Embellish tag with charms hung from safety pin; attach to ribbon wrapped around tag. Adhere torn inked strip to top and vellum quote at bottom; tie off with ribbon and mount on page.

Laura Swinson, Pearland, Texas

Adore

Stitch a journaling border

Give added impact to journaling by framing it inside a torn cardstock block with stitched sides to form a border. Begin with a textured olive cardstock background. Cut section from textured black cardstock for journaling frame; tear out center. Journal on tan cardstock; cut out, crumple, flatten and layer on page beneath black frame. Machine stitch around journaling. Tie charm with raffia; adhere on journaling frame. Mat photo on black cardstock; adhere on page. Accent with definition printed on tan cardstock strip; affix with black brads. Adhere strip of textured black cardstock under photo across page. Finish with metal letters for title.

Teresa L. Olier, Colorado Springs, Colorado

Supplies: Textured green and black cardstocks (Bazzill); metal alphabet letters (Making Memories); charm (source unknown); tan cardstock; raffia; black brads

Blessed

*Alter an envelope to hold
a special letter*

Write a heartfelt letter to a loved one and
tuck it safely away inside an altered envelope. Mat black patterned paper on a
black cardstock background. Cut small
section from patterned paper; mount to
bottom corner. Mount section of green
patterned paper on page. Cut two strips
from black cardstock; adhere vertically
on left side of page, weaving one strip
under gingham ribbon attached along
bottom of green paper. Mount photo.
Print title onto green cardstock; cut out
and ink edges in orange. Mat on black
cardstock and affix to page. Cover small
manila envelope in green floral patterned
paper; trim off excess and sand edges.
Cover flap of envelope with script paper;
trim excess and embellish with flower
sticker. Affix envelope to page and place
letter inside to finish.

Melissa Predmore, Aloha, Oregon

*Supplies: Textured black and green cardstocks (Bazzill); patterned papers (7 Gypsies, KI Memo-
ries); flower sticker (EK Success); orange ink; gingham ribbon; small manila envelope*

*Supplies: Patterned papers (7 Gypsies, Creative Imaginations); definition sticker, metal accents (Making
Memories); love poem stone (Creative Imaginations); speckled cardstock; black and silver brads; brown ink*

Dream Boy

Dedicate a layout to your husband

Take an opportunity to show your husband how
much he means to you by dedicating a layout to
him. Begin with a green cardstock background;
border bottom with script patterned paper treated
with brown ink. Adhere cut section from green
patterned paper to page. Alter photos slightly
in a photo-editing software program; print, mat
and adhere to page. Print journaling on speckled
cardstock; cut out and ink edges with brown
ink. Mat journaling on patterned paper; adhere
between photos. Ink edges of definition sticker
brown and mat on black cardstock block, leaving
room at right for metal embellishments. Add metal
heart adhered with silver brad and metal "boy"
word. Print additional journaling onto speckled
cardstock. Cut into strips for bottom border; ink,
mat on black cardstock and mount on page with
black brads. Finish with "love" poem stone applied
at bottom right corner.

Keisha Campbell, Great Lakes, Illinois

My Sweetie

Scrapbook your term of endearment

Document the pet name you and your significant other have for one another for a fun love layout. Cut sections of green patterned paper; treat edges with black ink. Layer black cardstock background with sections of red and patterned papers. Tear center from tan cardstock for frame. Roll torn edges; treat with brown ink and color on "mitered" corners. Stamp keys in red ink; heat-set with clear embossing powder. Mat photo on brown cardstock; affix frame atop photo. Emboss metal tag with several layers of mixed colored powders; punch rectangles from ends. String gingham ribbon through; wrap around frame, adding brads at top and bottom. Ink metal letter in red; emboss with clear embossing powder and adhere to tag. Journal on ivory cardstock; chalk edges in mustard and brown. Attach ribbon and brads around corners; mount on page. Cut tag from tan cardstock; cut out section for pocket and machine stitch strips of red and ivory cardstock on edge. Machine stitch around tag edge to create pocket. Stamp key on rustic heart; clear emboss and affix inside tag pocket. Attach tab made from brown cardstock covered with gingham ribbon and secured with brad. Embellish with heart and red wire attached with brad; mount tag to page. Use letter stickers to apply title.

Stacy Yoder, Yucaipa, California

Supplies: Patterned papers (All My Memories, Karen Foster Design, 7 Gypsies); key stamp (Club Scrap); metal letter and tag (Making Memories); rustic heart (Dizzy Frizzy); letter stickers (Creative Imaginations, EK Success); red, brown and tan cardstocks; red, brown and mustard inks; gingham ribbon; brads; red wire

My Love, My Life, My Husband

Give a gift bag additional purpose

Create an attractive page addition and pocket for journaling from a gift bag. Begin with a textured green cardstock background. Attach a thick gold ribbon vertically on left side of page. Double mat enlarged sepia-tinted photo on black cardstock and embossed sienna cardstock; adhere to right side of page. Cut front off gift bag and affix to page over ribbon, applying adhesive to bottom and side edges only to form a pocket for journaling. Journal on yellow cardstock tag; cut out and slip into bag. Reduce photos to fit behind slide mounts; cut out and affix to backs. Mount slide-framed photos atop gift bag to complete.

Martha Crowther, Salem, New Hampshire

Supplies: Textured green cardstock (source unknown); embossed sienna cardstock (Club Scrap); gift bag (Target); black cardstock; black slide mounts (Pakon); ribbon

Believe

Create a pocket-sized album for your page

Capture sweet moments with photos and record them in a photojournaling book. Begin with two patterned terracotta background pages. For left page, layer torn green patterned paper, photo background strip and torn vellum to create border; machine stitch all together onto page. Add knots created from tan shoelaces for embellishments. Cut title from patterned paper with a craft knife; mount on border strip, adding punched flower with wire center embellishment. Mat focal photo on terracotta mat; affix to page. For journaling book, use several 4 x 6" pages for journaling and additional photos. Create cover by adhering patterned paper over front of top page; line up pages and lace with jute through eyelets. Run a photo through an adhesive-application machine. Print quote on vellum, mount atop photo and accent with knotted shoelace. Mount book on page. For flower-embellished square, machine stitch patterned paper to light green cardstock. Layer several torn scraps on bottom of square; adorn with punched flowers, wire and eyelets. For right page, mount sepia-tinted focal photo on green patterned paper mat. Tint flower in photo with pens. Make peekaboo frame from patterned paper; affix over photo, adding flower embellishments made from punched scraps and wire. Double mat smaller photo on green and patterned papers; adhere to page. Mat remaining photo on two-sided green patterned paper. Cut slits in corners; fold edges over and machine sew. Adorn frame with knotted shoelaces and knotted patterned paper strips. Fashion name tag from layered patterned paper and printed vellum; attach with orange eyelets.

Cathy Lucas, Oro Valley, Arizona

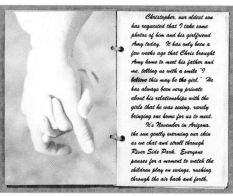

Supplies: Patterned paper, vellum (Chatterbox); photo border strip (source unknown); jute; wire; flower punches; white and terracotta eyelets; tan shoelaces

Integrity

Design an earthy layout

Create a rustic collage with organic elements for an eye-catching page. Begin by layering sections of patterned and mulberry papers on an orange cardstock background. Print quote onto orange cardstock; mat on gray cardstock, leaving room at left side for embellishments. Tear off edge; wrap with fiber and embellish with buttons and dried leaves. Mat photo on gray cardstock; adhere with matted quote onto page. Tear corner piece from cork sheet; embellish edge with fibers and mount in corner of page. Apply letter stickers on torn gray and orange cardstock mats; chalk torn edges in dark orange and mount on cork section. Embellish page with copper coastal netting, buttons, dried leaves and metal circle tag accented with fibers, wooden letter stickers and leaf. Stamp title onto gray cardstock; adhere on page.

Valerie Barton, Flowood, Mississippi

Supplies: Patterned paper (Glad Tidings); mulberry paper (Graphic Products); dried leaves (Pressed Petals); cork sheet, copper coastal netting (Magic Scraps); wooden letter stickers (EK Success); letter stamps (Hero Arts); orange and gray cardstocks; buttons; metal circle tag; fibers

Just To Make You Feel

Incorporate a song excerpt

Sometimes quoting the creative words of others is the perfect way to embody our feelings. Begin with a striped patterned paper background; treat edges with brown ink. Print photo in sepia tone; mat on tan cardstock, ink edges in brown and adhere on page. Cut sections from ephemera papers, ink edges in brown and mount on bottom of page. Tear top and bottom from tan cardstock section; ink torn edges in brown. Handwrite a portion of song lyrics and affix on center of page. Mount cut-out letters for first part of title on upper right side of page. Apply tag stickers for remaining title on bottom of page. Embellish photo with word sticker.

Jlyne Hanback, Biloxi, Mississippi
Lyrics: Bob Dylan

Supplies: Patterned paper (Chatterbox); ephemera papers (www.alteredpages.com); cut-out letters (Designer's Library); tag stickers (Sticker Studio); tan cardstock; brown ink

Cherish

Fashion a fun tag border

Put a new spin on a scrapbooking staple by linking tags together for a fresh page border. Begin with a textured brown cardstock background; heavily ink edges of cut script patterned paper in brown and mount along right side. Cut strip of handmade paper; affix horizontally across bottom of page. Print photo with white border; adhere on page. Weave cream ribbon through tag openings; adhere on left side of page. Mount metal plaque, metal letter, inked definition and letter stickers to tags to embellish.

Shelby Valadez, Saugus, California

Supplies: Textured brown cardstock (Bazzill); patterned paper (7 Gypsies); handmade paper (Artistic Scrapper); aged and distressed tags (2DYE4); metal plaque, metal letter, definition sticker (Making Memories); letter stickers (SEI); brown ink; cream ribbon

The Measure of A Man

Scrapbook his own unique standards

Celebrate how perfectly he measures up just the way he is. Begin with a textured light brown cardstock background. Tear the corner from textured dark brown cardstock; treat edge with black ink and adhere on corner of background. Mount cut patterned paper section on page. Alter a large tape measure sticker by sanding and adhere along left side of page. Print journaling onto cork sheet; cut out and mount on page with silver eyelets. Sand edges of photo and mat on dark brown cardstock; affix small sanded tape measure sticker to bottom. Adhere matted photo to page. Apply year on page with tag stickers attached with brads. Print statistics on tan cardstock; cut out, chalk edges in brown and adhere on page with eyelets. Apply title with a variety of stickers and letters cut out from dark brown cardstock; outline cardstock word with black ink.

Maegan Hall, Virginia Beach, Virginia

Supplies: Textured tan and dark brown cardstocks (Bazzill); patterned paper (7 Gypsies); type key letter stickers, tape measure and tag stickers (EK Success); additional letter stickers (Provo Craft); cork (Magic Scraps); tan brads; eyelets; chalk

JS

Celebrate your anniversary

Pay a tribute to your marriage with a layout celebrating your relationship. Treat a textured ivory cardstock background with a brown ink pad. Spray beige paper with walnut ink; layer onto background with cut sections of patterned papers that have been inked with brown ink pad. Adhere enlarged photo. Print enlarged initials onto textured green cardstock and journaling onto ivory cardstock; cut out, ink edges with brown ink pad and adhere onto page. Adorn journaling with metal heart eyelet.

Shelby Valadez, Saugus, California

Supplies: Textured cardstock (Bazzill); patterned papers (Anna Griffin, K & Company, 7 Gypsies); metal heart eyelet (Making Memories); brown ink; walnut ink

Cherish

Detail a layout with definitions of love

Yours is the definition of love—incorporate the literal ones as well for easy romantic page accents. Begin with a patterned paper background. Tear strip from black cardstock; adhere to right side of page. Double mat photo on gold and black cardstocks; wrap corners with fibers and mount on page. For journaling block, print journaling on vellum; double mat on gold and black cardstocks and affix to page. Mat definition sticker on gold cardstock; wrap left side with fiber and mount at askew angle on black cardstock strip. Affix various definitions to page. Print "love" on tan cardstock; cut out and adhere under label holder to page. Embellish remainder of page with poem stones, coins and clock hand.

Misty Posey, Decatur, Alabama

Supplies: Patterned paper (Scrap Ease); metallic gold cardstock (Bazzill); poem stones (Creative Imaginations); definition stickers (Making Memories); clock hand, label holder (Hot Off The Press); black cardstock; vellum; fibers; coins

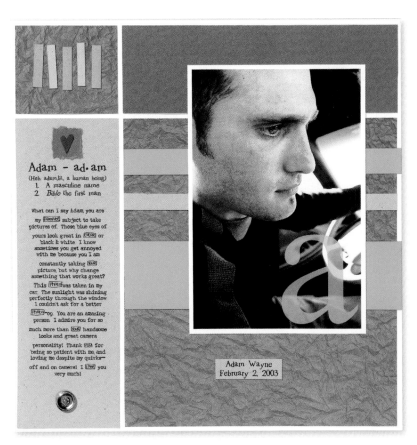

Supplies: *Patterned paper (Karen Foster Design); heart punch (EK Success); blue and gray cardstocks; heart button*

Adam

Feature a profile shot

"Profile" a special person with a single striking photo and meaningful journaling. Mount cut sections of gray cardstock and patterned paper on a white cardstock background page. Adhere strips of blue and light gray cardstocks on patterned paper sections. Use photo-editing software to apply letter on bottom of photo; print with white border and adhere on background page. Journal on light gray cardstock; cut and affix to page. Embellish bottom of journaling block with decorative silver button and top with torn gray cardstock square and punched heart. Print caption on light gray cardstock; mount below photo.

Rebecca Cantu, Brownwood, Texas

Supplies: *Patterned paper, label holder (Club Scrap); letter stickers (Creative Imaginations); tan and sienna cardstocks; fibers*

If

Journal loving thoughts

Make heartfelt journaling inspired by a significant other the central focus of a love-inspired layout. Begin with a blue patterned paper background. Print journaling on tan patterned paper; tear out and mat on sienna cardstock. Wrap fibers around each edge of journaling block, securing on back. Adhere to page. Mat photo on sienna cardstock; cut slits into corners and slip corners of photo inside. Adhere to tan cardstock mat and mount on page. Apply letter stickers to tan cardstock for title; cut out and affix to page under label holder with black brads.

Clara Hulsey, Dayton, Texas
Photo: Donna Manning, Huntsville, Texas

Supplies: Textured light blue cardstock (Bazzill); suede trim (Crafter's Workshop); small wreath (source unknown); tan and dark blue cardstocks; vellum; gold brads

There Are No Words

Print sentiments onto a photo

A great way to artfully express your feelings for a special someone in your scrapbook pages is to feature loving words over his or her photo. Begin with a brown cardstock background. Cut sections from light blue cardstocks and mount to page; add suede trim to top half of page. Print journaling on tan cardstock, leaving extra room at top and bottom. Adhere to page with gold brads. Affix suede trim across bottom of page. Mat cropped photo on dark blue cardstock; mount on bottom of journaling box. Accent top of journaling box with small wreath. Use Adobe Photoshop 7.0 to apply words directly onto focal photo; enlarge, print out, trim and adhere to page. Print title on vellum; cut out and attach over photo with brads.

Mellette Berezoski, Crosby, Texas

Love

Create a coastal feel

Use a sanding technique combined with a pre-made frame to give a beach-house feel to your coastal layout. Begin by treating edge of textured yellow cardstock background with blue and metallic bronze ink. Layer sections torn and cut from patterned paper and sand-colored cardstock on background. Layer photo and premade wood frame onto left side of page; attach copper plate at bottom with copper brad on right side. Hang safety pins on left side. Sand along edges of remaining photo with sand-paper to mimic a frame. Print journaling onto blue cardstock. Create double mat for photo by cutting journaling and layering beneath white cardstock mat. Wrap with fiber and adhere to page. Treat tag accent with blue and metallic bronze inks; tie off with fibers and embellish with torn patterned paper corner piece. Print journaling onto vellum; cut out and wrap around tag. Adorn with faux wax seal and adhere to page. Alter metal "love" word using copper metallic rub-ons; cover in pearl embossing powder and heat to set. Adhere on page. Mount watch crystal over sand and shell collected from beach. Stamp date to finish.

Lindsay Teague, Phoenix, Arizona

Supplies: Textured yellow cardstock (Bazzill); patterned paper (Autumn Leaves); wood frame (Cropper Hopper); copper memories plate (K & Company); safety pins, metal word (Making Memories); faux wax seal (Creative Imaginations); copper metallic rub-ons (Craf-T); pearl embossing powder; watch crystal (Scrapworks); date stamp (Office Max); blue and metallic bronze inks; sand-colored cardstock; tag; vellum; fibers; beach sand and shell

The Dance Of Life

Supplies: Clip Art (Broderbund); peach, white and green cardstocks; sheet music; peach chalk; matte photo paper

Compose your own music-patterned paper

Creating a custom background is easy with the use of a scanner, sheet music and clip art. Begin with two peach-colored cardstock background pages. For musical background papers, scan a piece of sheet music; print along with musical clip art. Treat with peach and pink chalks; re-scan chalked images and print onto matte photo paper. Layer cut and torn pieces to form a collage background; adhere to peach background pages. Alter collage papers with white ink where desired for muted effect. Print photos with white borders; mat on green cardstock and adhere to pages. Print title, journaling and caption on white cardstock; tear out, ink torn edges in peach and pink and adhere to pages.

Sharon Whitehead, Vernon, British Columbia, Canada

After 32 Years

Generate a computer layout without going digital

You don't have to be a whiz at photo-editing software to create a cutting-edge computer-generated layout. Try using a project-oriented software program to create a unique piece of artwork. Begin with a light blue cardstock background. Use Broderbund PrintMaster12 Gold to apply title, phrases and words that describe your relationship using different fonts. Decide placement of photos by bringing them into your project area and enlarging or reducing as desired. Print photos onto matte photo paper. Print out layout and add printed photos to predetermined locations.

Sharon Whitehead, Vernon, British Columbia, Canada

Supplies: Textured light blue cardstock (Bazzill); PrintMaster 12 Gold (Broderbund); matte photo paper

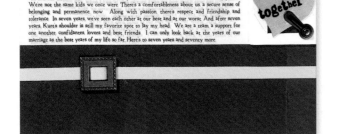

November 2003

Our Seventh Year

Muse on a single meaningful photo

Create a single-photo layout from a favorite shot that says it all. Begin with a textured dark blue cardstock background. Enlarge photo to fit horizontally across page; print with white border and adhere. Stamp date on white paper; cut out and affix over edge of photo. Add black photo turn with silver brad. Cut strip from white paper and adhere horizontally beneath photo. Print journaling on transparency and layer over white strip. Thread thin strip of textured light blue cardstock through charm and adhere across bottom of page. For slide embellishment, affix slide mount at the end of the white paper strip. Layer with metal heart and word printed on transparency. Snip ends from silver brads; adhere to transparency and heart and over black photo turn.

Angelina Schwarz, New Castle, Pennsylvania
Photo: Patricia Alexander, Lock Haven, Pennsylvania

Supplies: Textured blue cardstocks (Bazzill); ribbon charm (Making Memories); black photo turn (7 Gypsies); white slide mount (Pakon); date stamp; white paper; silver brads; transparency

Tom And Becky

Define your passions in a scrapbook page

Love-themed definition paper makes for a perfect backdrop for a photo of one of your shared passions. Begin with a textured blue cardstock background. Mount section of patterned paper across background page, leaving upper left corner un-adhered to form a pocket. Mount strips of black cardstock to top and bottom edges of patterned paper; add rivets to bottom strip. Mat photo on black cardstock, leaving room at right for title. Stamp title and adhere to page. Thread gingham ribbon through metal charm; mount across center of page. Cut tag from tan cardstock; detail with brown ink to age. Outline in black pen and journal your favorite activities as a couple. Adhere metal letter and tiny photo to top of tag; slide behind patterned paper.

Becky Novacek, Fremont, Nebraska

Supplies: Textured blue and black cardstocks (Bazzill); patterned paper (Carolee's Creations); letter stamps (Ma Vinci's); tan cardstock; ribbon charm, metal letter (Making Memories); rivets (Chatterbox); white and brown inks; gingham ribbon; black pen

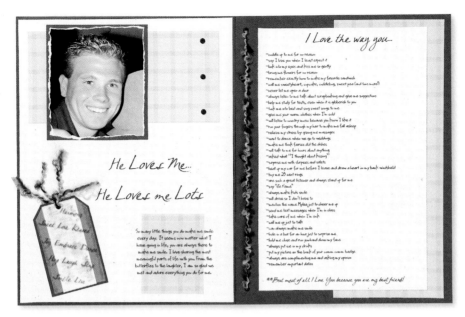

Supplies: Patterned paper (Lasting Impressions); cream fleck paper; white and blue cardstocks; blue eyelets; blue snaps; fiber

He Loves Me...He Loves Me Lots

Record the many ways he displays his devotion

Document all the details of the special ways he shows his love. Begin with two dark blue cardstock backgrounds. For left page, print title onto cream-colored fleck paper; mat on background. Mount two blocks of patterned paper to page; add blue snaps to top section. Tear photo; mat on blue cardstock and adhere over patterned paper. Journal on vellum; mount over patterned paper block. For tag, print words onto vellum; chalk and layer on white strip and blue cardstock tag. Set blue eyelet in top; tie off with fiber and mount on page. For right page, journal list on cream-colored fleck paper; trim and layer over patterned paper and adhere to background. Set blue eyelets at top and bottom corners of left side of page; string fiber through, securing to back of page.

Andrea Graves, Sandy, Utah

Dan

Assign a tag double duty

Create a collage-style accent and a journaling booklet all in one by connecting two tags. Begin with a black cardstock background. Adhere patterned paper to page; add section of additional patterned paper to bottom and small strip to top. Thread gingham ribbon through metal charm; adhere across top of patterned paper border. Print photo with white border; adhere to page with black photo corners. Use metallic rub-ons to alter metal word. Layer over crumpled and inked piece of patterned paper and tan leather strip; mount on page. For tag booklet, create "hinge" from cut piece of leather; fold over two tags and staple together. Accent with leather piece. Adhere bottom tag to page and journal inside. Apply title to top tag using a letter tile matted on black cardstock, letter stamps, definition, metal piece, epoxy letters and leather trim accent. For name feature, cut out letters and adhere under copper label holder. Affix small leather piece to top corner of page to finish.

Sherri Winstead, Fayetteville, North Carolina

Supplies: Patterned papers (Provo Craft, 7 Gypsies); black photo corners (Canson); metal word, ribbon charm, definitions (Making Memories); metallic rub-ons (Craf-T); leather (Crafter's Workshop); letter tile (Westrim); letter stamps (PSX Design); epoxy words, bookplate, circle metal (Li'l Davis Designs); cut-out letters (Foofala); black cardstock; brown tags; staples; safety pin; black ink

Love

Feature a special photo

Keep the layout simple when you want the focus to stay on a meaningful photo. Begin by treating the edges of a textured brown cardstock background with dark brown ink; print names and date on bottom corner. Cut section from patterned paper; tear top and bottom edges and treat with dark brown ink. Double mat photo on brown cardstock and wood-grained patterned paper treated with brown ink; layer onto page with patterned paper section. Wrap fibers around center of layout; secure beneath copper "love" plate adhered to page with foam adhesive.

Kelli Lawlor, Norfolk, Virginia

Supplies: Textured brown cardstock (Bazzill); wood-grained paper (Karen Foster Design); patterned paper (7 Gypsies); copper "love" plate (Global Solutions); dark brown ink; fibers

One Fine Day

Utilize clip art accents

Print just the right clip art onto transparencies to add a finishing touch to a page. Begin by adhering patterned vellum on a teal paper background. Scan fountain pen clip art into Adobe Photoshop 7.0; re-size as desired and print along with title and journaling onto transparencies. Mount on page. Mat photos on darker teal cardstock; mount on page. Affix foreign postage stamps on teal cardstock; cut out with decorative scissors and adhere on page with foam adhesive.

Kari Hansen-Daffin, Memory Makers magazine

Supplies: Patterned vellum (Paper Adventures); Photoshop (Adobe); decorative scissors (Fiskars); teal paper; teal cardstock; transparency; foam adhesive; clip art (source unknown)

Tom

Use bead words for added emphasis

Put a new twist on journaling by stringing bead words into your sentences. Begin with a red patterned paper background. Layer torn strips of red and black patterned papers to page. Cover left side of page with cropped black-and-white photos. Border the edges of the photos with gingham ribbon. Crop portion from original color photo and adhere to back of slide mount frame covered with red patterned paper and embelllished with glossy accent; mount on matching photo with foam adhesive. Stamp title on white cardstock; cut out, treat with black ink and mount under red label holder with red brads. Journal on white cardstock; leave room to add bead words. Cut into strips; treat with black ink and adhere to background page. Affix beads to strips and thread with red floss. Finish by hand stitching X's at random along strips with red floss.

Jodi Amidei, Memory Makers Books

Supplies: Patterned papers (Carolee's Creations); slide mount (Design Originals); glossy accent (Ranger); red label holder (Li'l Davis Designs); beads (Magnetic Poetry); letter stamps (Stampin' Up!); white cardstock; gingham ribbon; red brads; black ink; red floss

To My Sweetheart

Celebrate your anniversary
with a look back in time

Craft an anniversary layout that pays tribute to both the present and the past with a flip page. Begin by machine stitching brown paper strips to the top and bottom of a tan patterned paper background page. Print photo caption, title and journaling onto vellum. Cut out, treat edges with watermark ink and brush with copper pigment powder. Wrap vellum caption strip and sheer copper ribbon around "past" photo. Add metal charm to ribbon and adhere to page. Affix angular scraps to cardstock panel to form background for journaling block. Layer with journaled vellum. Stamp heart and key images with watermark ink; brush with copper pigment powder. Accent title with tortoise shell frame; mount to page above journaling. To create flip page, machine stitch brown paper and cream cardstock together. Mount tan patterned paper to interior side. Create a pocket for love letters from a panel of patterned paper adhered to background and trimmed with ribbon. Repeat journaling block technique for the front of pocket. Attach flip page by bending left edge of brown paper over left edge of background page; secure with adhesive. Mount recent photo; add tortoise shell corners, vellum caption, metal charm and sheer ribbons to photo.

Pamela James, Ventura, California

Supplies: Tan patterned paper (My Mind's Eye); watermark ink (Tsukineko); copper pigment powder (Ranger); tortoise shell frames and corners, metal charms (K & Company); heart and key stamps (Close To My Heart); brown paper; vellum; cream cardstock; sheer copper ribbon

cherish (cher·ish) 1. to hold dear 2. to treasure, adore, value and love 2. to keep deeply in mind

family

loved

together

forever

Family

Family is everything, at least it is to me. I'm sure that as I was growing up, I was the type of teenager that my parents couldn't stand to be around & they probably thought I'd never turn out OK. But now that I am an adult, I am very close to my parents & consider them to also be amongst my closest friends & I talk & see them several times a week. See, I did turn out OK in the end.

FAMILY

is

eveRyThing

Christmas 2002

Family Matters □

No other faces appear as frequently within the pages of scrapbooks as those of family members. Celebrating us at our best, supporting us at our worst and sustaining us during all else in between, one of life's few true constants is family. It is no wonder that in all the milestones and precious moments, the presence of our family members makes our special memories complete. As adults our roles within the family evolve, whether we are beginning to add our own branches to the family tree, are forming grown-up friendships with our siblings and parents, or are just coming to recognize our roots through family fables, history and heritage. Scrapbook pages provide a snapshot-in-time glimpse into our unique family units. They chronicle the qualities we admire in notorious family "characters," capture the details of classic family gatherings and pay precious tribute to those we hold most dear. Whatever form your family takes, create a lasting keepsake for yours and future generations to cherish.

Established 2002

Feature a stencil as an embellishment

Include a lettering stencil of the first letter of your family name for a unique page accent. Begin with a khaki-colored cardstock background. Mount sections of patterned paper and vellum to page. Cut out tag and apply title with letter stamps and stickers. Affix title to vellum block with yellow ribbon. Adhere photo to page. Treat stencil with brown ink; adorn with heart token. Adhere to page over gold mesh; add last name created with label maker. Stamp names onto cut-out ID tags; mount on page with antique scrapbook tacks. Add "family" with stickers to bottom of page. Journal onto background.

Melanie Bauer, Columbia, Missouri

Supplies: Patterned paper, patterned vellum, letter stickers, cut-outs, antique scrapbook tacks (Chatterbox); letter stamps (Hero Arts); gold mesh (Magic Mesh); heart token (Doodlebug Design); khaki cardstock; label maker (Dymo); letter stencil; black pen

Supplies: Patterned paper, patterned vellum, antique flower tacks, date stickers (Chatterbox); handmade paper (Magenta); brown and rose tags (2DYE4); puffy letter stickers (K & Company); green cardstock; green ribbon; red chalk

Through Our Love

Enlarge a photo for added impact

Enlarge a vertical photo lengthwise for a striking panoramic effect. Begin with a light green cardstock background. Layer cut patterned vellum and patterned paper on page. Double mat photo on white cardstock and handmade paper; mount on background. Print full-length photo in panoramic mode. Tear right edge off photo; chalk in red and adhere to left side of page. Journal on brown tag and layer on tag. Add antique flower tacks in corner and green ribbon on end. Adhere to upper right corner of page. Apply date stickers on bottom corner of page.

Candi Gershon, Fishers, Indiana
Photos: Simone Steffensen, Palm Bay, Florida

Family Is The Key To Happiness

Mimic photo elements for a background

Re-create elements from your photo for your page background to create visual interest. Begin by painting sections of mesh with brown acrylic paint; mount on center of brown cardstock background page. Adhere cut section of brick patterned paper on bottom of page. Affix enlarged photo over left side of page. Print journaling on patterned vellum; tear top edge and adhere on bottom of page with copper brads. Tear small sections from textured green cardstock; emboss edges with clear powder and layer on upper right corner of page. Apply title by cutting out first part using lettering template and blue and ivory cardstocks; affix to page. Apply remainder of title with leather letter stickers adhered over torn and rolled ivory and tan cardstock strips; affix to page. Embellish page with key accents.

Jennifer Bourgeault, Macomb Township, Michigan

Supplies: Mesh (Magic Mesh); brown acrylic paint (Plaid); brick patterned paper (Club Scrap); patterned vellum (It Takes Two); textured green cardstock (Bazzill); clear embossing powder (Stampendous); lettering template (Wordsworth); leather letter stickers (All My Memories); keys (Li'l Davis designs); brown cardstock; copper brads

Mom & Me

Craft faux soldered frames

Create the unique look of soldered frames and matching star accents with a melting pot. Begin by printing journaling along bottom of rust cardstock; mat on gray cardstock and mount on black cardstock background. Punch star shape in scrap cardstock; adhere with temporary adhesive to background and apply sepia ink with stipple brush. Treat section of handmade paper with metallic steel paint; immediately spray with magic metal rapid rust. Set with sealant. Shape right corners with corner punch; adhere paper to right side of page. Cut sections from patterned paper; coat with several layers of extra thick embossing powder. When cool, bend to crack; affix on page. Mat all photos on gray cardstock; double mat top photo on black cardstock and mount photos on page. For title, stamp letters for first part of title on patterned paper pieces; dip edges in melting pot containing melted platinum and clear extra thick embossing powder to create faux soldered frame. For second part of title, sandwich stamped letters between microscope slides; dip edges into pot and mount on page. Repeat melting pot technique to alter star brads; affix on page.

Torrey Miller, Thornton, Colorado

Supplies: Patterned paper (K & Company); handmade paper (source unknown); star brads (Magic Scraps); watermark ink (Tsukineko); platinum and clear extra thick embossing powders (Ranger); magic metallic paint, rapid rust and sealant (Coloramics); letter stamps (Hampton Art); melting pot (Ranger); rust, gray and black cardstocks; microscope slides; star punch; sepia ink

Supplies: Textured brown and tan cardstocks (Bazzill); patterned paper (K & Company); rub-on word, metal letters, page pebble (Making Memories); pointing finger, tape measure, and letter stickers (EK Success); letter stickers (Creative Imaginations); tag stickers, mini envelope (DMD); label maker (Dymo); clock face embellishment (source unknown); black ink

Growing Up Together

Showcase "then" and "now" shots

Pay tribute to past and present family times on a page that measures the ways you've changed. Begin with a textured brown cardstock background; treat edges with black ink. Adhere various inked patterned papers to page. Scan old and current photos and print in black-and-white with white borders. Ink edges of photos in black. Tear top from old photo; mat both photos on tan cardstock mats with edges treated with black ink. Adhere the corner from a piece of patterned paper to recent photo; wrap photos with fiber and mount both on page. Add "life" rub-on word directly to photo. Adhere small date tags to photos. Apply pointing finger sticker to top right corner; top with label. Apply tape measure sticker over upper left corner of torn photo. Apply title to bottom left corner using various metal letters, stickers, page pebble and label. Mat metal letters with tan cardstock squares treated with black ink. Use a variety of nostalgic sticker tags to mat sticker letters and page pebble. Slip left end of label title into small envelope that has been treated with black ink; mount to page. Apply sticker tag next to label; embellish with clock face embellishment to finish page.

Elizabeth Cuzzacrea, Lockport, New York

Love You

Incorporate handwritten letters

Tell your dad what he means to his family with letters written to him from you and the grandchildren. Begin with a tan cardstock background; treat edges with black ink. Tear right edge from green cardstock; adhere over tan cardstock background bending top left corner. Cut section from patterned paper; treat edges with black ink and adhere to page. Create envelope for letter from patterned paper; treat edges with black ink and mount to page. Make envelope embellishments with large antique eyelets set into small circles punched from tan cardstock; adhere to top and bottom of envelope along with waxed cording and metal phrase. Double mat focal photo on brown cardstock and patterned paper; treat with ink and affix to page. Adhere "success" tag and metal "father" word on photo and mat. Apply title with letter squares and typewriter stickers adhered to stitched metal circles. Punch heart from red cardstock; slide into metal label holder and adhere to page. Have grandchildren journal on tag; slip into bag and adhere to page. Apply grandfather pebble sticker to top of bag.

Cindy Harris, Modesto, California

Supplies: Patterned papers (7 Gypsies); title squares (My Mind's Eye); letter stickers (EK Success); stitched metal circles, label holder, metal words and phrase (Making Memories); tag in a bag (DMD); pebble sticker (Creative Imaginations); success tag (Me & My Big Ideas); tan, green, brown and red cardstocks; black ink; large antique eyelets; heart punch

Memories

Emphasize a cropped photo element

To emphasize a particular portion from your photo, layer a section cropped from a color print over a black-and-white copy and accent it with a metal frame. Begin by treating the edges of a textured brown cardstock background with black ink. Alter edges of cut patterned paper sections with black ink; adhere on background. Stamp clock image on bottom of page. Print journaling onto a transparency; cut out and affix over patterned paper. Affix strip of gingham paper over edge of transparency; stamp on date. Sand edges of black-and-white photo copy; ink in black and mount on page. Crop section from color photo, mount on back of metal frame and adhere on top of black-and-white photo. Stamp name onto frame in black ink. Stamp clock image over corner of photo and onto patterned paper. Treat definition stickers with walnut ink and ink edges in black; adhere on page. Stamp names of people in photo onto background.

Jlyne Hanback, Biloxi, Mississippi

Supplies: Textured brown cardstock (Bazzill); patterned papers (7 Gypsies); clock stamp (source unknown); letter stamps (Hero Arts); metal frame, definition stickers (Making Memories); solvent-based black ink for metal frame (Tsukineko); walnut ink

Fabric Of Our Lives

Feature fabrics for a texture-rich layout

Here siblings are celebrated on a page comprised of fabric swatches, stitching and fine design. Begin with a red cardstock background. Machine stitch floral fabric to background page. Trim opposite corners from piece of red fabric; machine stitch to page. Machine stitch ribbon diagonally across top of red fabric. Double mat photos on yellow fabric and strips of cardstock folded in half. Machine stitch folded strips on inside flap across center of page. Affix corresponding photos from past on inside of flaps. Cut section away from red fabric and page for journaling. Print journaling on yellow cardstock; cut out and affix on back side of page over opening. Machine stitch around journaling opening. Adhere decorative metal corners to page. Embellish edges of page with diamond brads. Cut first part of title using a craft knife and a computer font as a guide from yellow and red cardstocks; adhere to top of page. Mount metal letters on ribbon for second part of title.

Shannon Taylor, Bristol, Tennessee

Supplies: Ribbon, decorative metal corners and diamond brads (Magic Scraps); metal letters (Making Memories); red and yellow cardstocks; floral, red and yellow fabrics

Cherish

Combine rich colors and patterns

Blend bold, deep colors, complementary patterns and emotion-rich journaling for a touching page about family. Begin with a floral-patterned paper background; layer dark floral and green patterned paper sections over background. Slide ribbon charm onto ivory ribbon; attach on page beneath patterned paper and secondary photo. Ink edges of definition sticker in black and attach on page with silver eyelets. Ink edges of jewelry tag, stamp on date and string with fiber; thread through eyelets securing on back of page. Journal directly onto page to complete.

Vicki Chrisman, North Bend, Nebraska

Supplies: Patterned papers (Anna Griffin, Daisy D's); ribbon charm, definition sticker (Making Memories); date stamp (Staples); black ink; silver eyelets; jewelry tag; fibers; ribbon

Supplies: Brown handmade paper (Book By Hand/Solum); patterned paper (Anna Griffin, DMD); decoupage adhesive (USArtQuest); hinges (Stanley Classic Brassware); decorative photo corners (Jesse James); silver pendant, brass oval frame, charms (Beads & Plenty More); crystal lacquer (Stampin' Up!); letter stickers (Creative Imaginations); artificial flowers (Card Connection); ivory cardstock; gold fibers; beads; buttons; lace fabric; stick pins

A Drawer Full Of Memories

Mimic the look of a memorabilia drawer

Create an assortment of treasures you might find exploring Grandma's keepsake drawers. Begin by adhering brown handmade paper and patterned paper on heavy cardstock with decoupage adhesive. Distress several collage paper elements with sandpaper and chalks to age; layer over background. For "album" cover, alter a photo mat by bending it and embossing it on edges with gold powder. Wrap gold ribbon around frame; tie to side and accent with beads. Adhere photo on backside of cover. Tear edges of patterned paper and emboss with gold powder; adhere to back of album cover. To form interior, layer cardboard backing from photo mat to page background; layer with torn and gold-embossed patterned paper and journaling passage. Glue hinges to cardboard backing and album cover. Embellish corners of cover with gold accents. Adhere oval frame to bottom; apply stickers inside and cover with crystal lacquer. Apply title to page background with letter stickers. Mount decorative sticker inside silver pendant and fill with crystal effects; tie with fiber and adhere on page. Embellish page with additional collage elements such as buttons, charms, lace and artificial flowers with stick pins.

Colleen Macdonald, Calgary, Alberta, Canada

Salt Of
The Earth

Create a temporary photo frame

If you have a special photo that you don't wish to adhere permanently to your page, create a sewn vellum slip-in frame for an artistic solution. Begin with a chestnut cardstock background page. Cut a strip from corrugated paper from which to "hang" tags; attach ends to page with brads. Emboss metal letters and metal-rimmed tag for title with copper extra thick embossing powder. Cut tags from ivory cardstock; ink edges and stamp with wheat and texture images in brown ink. Stamp letters to form title on individual tags; add embossed letters and hang from corrugated strip with floss. Create photo mat by machine stitching corners of torn patterned vellum to brown cardstock; slide photo inside. Journal on ivory cardstock; cut into rectangle, ink edges, stamp images, add stitched buttons and mount on vellum frame.

Colleen Adams, Huntington Beach, California
Photo: Sarah Schue, St. Paul, Minnesota

Supplies: Corrugated paper, patterned vellum, wheat and texture stamp (Club Scrap); metal letters, metal-rimmed vellum tag (Making Memories); copper extra thick embossing powder (Ranger); letter stamps (PSX Design); chestnut, and brown and ivory cardstocks; brads; floss; black and brown inks

Heritage

Celebrate your unique roots

Age symbolic elements for a striking page that pays tribute to your heritage. Begin by covering cardstock with cut pieces of patterned paper; ink and chalk edges in brown and adhere. Journal on tan cardstock; ink and chalk edges in brown. Roll edges slightly, mat on patterned paper mat and adhere on page. Create journaling tags from patterned papers; age by crumpling, inking and chalking in brown. Cover tag layered with map paper with decoupage adhesive. Tie off tags with leather strips and adhere to top of page, securing leather strips on back. Adhere beaded accents on second tag. Print title onto brown cardstock; crumple, iron, then add color detail with blue chalk. Cut out, machine stitch onto brown chipboard and coat with decoupage adhesive. Adhere to page. Create faux envelope from patterned paper; chalk to age. Attach leather strips; string beads and attach charm. Print quotes on tan cardstock; cut out, chalk and adhere on envelope and right side of page. Affix pewter corners on envelope and page. Copy cultural image onto ivory cardstock; cut out, color with chalks and cover in decoupage adhesive. Adhere on page. Alter brads and plate with antiquing solvent and affix to page. Finish with tied feather charm in upper corner.

Linda Albrecht, St. Peter, Minnesota

Supplies: Patterned papers (K & Company, Provo Craft); silver beaded buttons and tree (Hobby Lobby); decoupage adhesive (Plaid); pewter photo corners (Pewter Accents); turtle charm and beads (Bead Treasures); metal tag (Making Memories); antiquing solvent (Modern Options); fibers; feather; brown ink; brown chalk

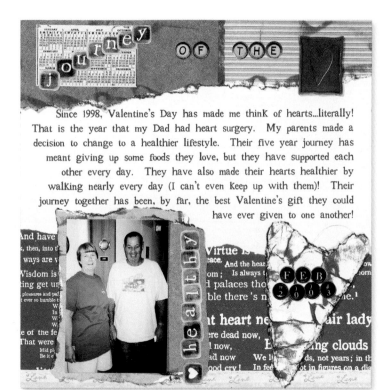

Since 1998, Valentine's Day has made me think of hearts...literally! That is the year that my Dad had heart surgery. My parents made a decision to change to a healthier lifestyle. Their five year journey has meant giving up some foods they love, but they have supported each other every day. They have also made their hearts healthier by walking nearly every day (I can't even keep up with them!) Their journey together has been, by far, the best Valentine's gift they could have ever given to one another!

Journey Of The Heart

Journal an accomplishment

Document a monumental decision, such as deciding to commit to a healthier lifestyle, with a special layout. Journal directly onto an ivory cardstock background page. Tear brown patterned paper for top border; treat torn edges with brown ink and adhere to top of page. Affix calendar sticker in top corner; apply title with letter stickers. Embellish with heart plaque. Tear black patterned paper for bottom border; adhere and machine stitch "love" bias tape onto bottom. Mat photo on torn and inked sections of patterned paper; embellish with heart and letter stickers. Adhere matted photo to page. Tear heart from ivory cardstock; crumple, flatten, ink in brown and adhere to page. Apply date to heart with letter stickers.

Pam Canavan, Clermont, Florida

Supplies: Patterned papers (Carolee's Creations, 7 Gypsies); letter stickers (Creative Imaginations, EK Success); calendar sticker (EK Success); heart stamp (PSX Design); love bias tape (Wrights); heart plaque (Making Memories); ivory cardstock

Life Is God's Gift To You

Reflect upon a stressful time

Recalling a near-fatal health problem in your scrapbook can be a therapeutic way to reflect and re-evaluate the meaning of life. Begin with a rust cardstock background. Journal on crackle patterned paper; cut out and adhere to page. Tear and affix section from yellow patterned paper for bottom border. Affix gingham ribbon, gold embossed tile and square cropped photos on border. Mat focal photo on black cardstock, then mount on large yellow cardstock mat. Paint rust-colored acrylic paint on larger mat. Cut photo corners from yellow patterned paper; treat edges with black ink and attach with black brads on photo frame. Affix framed photo to page. Cut part of title from rust cardstock with a craft knife; affix on crackle paper, inking edges in black. Print remainder of title on yellow paper, leaving room for matted title piece; tear out and adhere complete title to page.

Chris Douglas, East Rochester, Ohio

Supplies: Patterned papers (Mustard Moon, Colorbök); embossed gold tile (Scrapyard 329); rust acrylic paint (Delta); rust and yellow cardstocks; gingham ribbon; black ink; black brads

One Man's Legacy

Showcase mini portraits

Do you have a photographer in the family? Show off his or her work by including reduced versions of some of their exceptional shots on a page. Begin by adhering sections of burgundy cardstock and textured tan cardstock to a black cardstock background. Enlarge and print focal photo with white border; mount on page. Scan in all photos and reduce to desired sizes; print, cut out and adhere to page. Use a laser die-cutting machine to cut letters from black and white cardstocks for title using various fonts and sizes. Mount on page.

Carey Johnson, St. Cloud, Minnesota

Supplies: Tan textured cardstock (Bazzill); circle punch (Fiskars); black, burgundy and white cardstocks

Supplies: Textured ivory cardstock (Bazzill); patterned papers (7 Gypsies, Paper Adventures, Scrap Ease); ribbon charm, definition sticker, rectangle clip (Making Memories); faith label (Me & My Big Ideas); letter tiles (Westrim); pewter leaf embellishment (Boutique Trims); walnut ink (7 Gypsies); brown ink; vellum; tan and brown acrylic paint; silver brads; ribbon

Believe

Reflect on conquering an illness

Incorporate an inspirational passage in a layout that deals with a loved one battling an illness. Begin by painting a textured ivory cardstock background with tan acrylic paint and a toothbrush. Tear various patterned papers; layer on page. Paint a definition sticker to match background; affix to upper corner. Alter patterned paper on bottom right corner with brown paint. Attach "faith" label with rectangle clipped onto photo; tuck into corner layer. Journal passage onto vellum; tear out, treat with brown ink and adhere to page with silver brads. Print caption on ivory cardstock; cut out, rub with brown ink, crumple, flatten and adhere above photo with silver brads. For tag accent, age tag with walnut ink; adhere title with letter tiles over torn paper piece. Thread brown ribbon through tag; adhere tag on page. Slide ribbon charm onto ribbon and adhere to page, securing around left edge. Affix pewter leaf to tag.

Elsa Duff, Whitecourt, Alberta, Canada

The World Is Your Oyster

Create a title overlay

Use a preprinted overlay to enhance your layout and to make applying a title a snap. Begin with two patterned paper backgrounds. Tint photos in sepia tone. Double mat recent photos on green and ivory cardstocks; ink edges of ivory mat in black and adhere on left page. Tie metal letter circle with black ribbon onto charm; wrap ribbon around inside of circle charm and secure around left side of page. Mount overlay on page. For right page, adhere older photos to center of background page. Journal on vellum and adhere over photos. Trim edge of vellum with black ribbon; slide ribbon charms onto bottom ribbon. Add decorative corners to top corners. Mount older photo inside metal frame on page.

Sue Fields, South Whitley, Indiana
Photos: Frederick's Photography, Huntington, Indiana

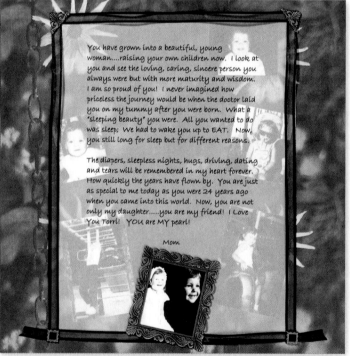

You have grown into a beautiful, young woman....raising your own children now. I look at you and see the loving, caring, sincere person you always were but with more maturity and wisdom. I am so proud of you! I never imagined how priceless the journey would be when the doctor laid you on my tummy after you were born. What a "sleeping beauty" you were. All you wanted to do was sleep; We had to wake you up to EAT. Now, you still long for sleep but for different reasons.

The diapers, sleepless nights, hugs, driving, dating and tears will be remembered in my heart forever. How quickly the years have flown by. You are just as special to me today as you were 24 years ago when you came into this world. Now, you are not only my daughter.....you are my friend! I Love You Torri! YOU are MY pearl!

Mom

Supplies: Patterned papers (Rusty Pickle); overlay (Artistic Expressions); decorative photo corners, circle charm, metal frame (K & Company); mini buckles (Making Memories); circle metal letter (Die Cuts With A View); vellum; green and ivory cardstocks; black ribbon

He's My Daddy

Use various fonts for visual interest

Print directly onto various colored cardstocks in a variety of fonts for an eye-appealing page. Begin with a textured blue cardstock background; adhere section of light blue textured cardstock on top of background. Use Broderbund software to arrange placement of words, title and photo. Print directly onto pieced page. Print title and words on textured purple cardstock; cut title and mount across page. Trim edges of title strip and one journaling block with black cardstock strips. Adhere gingham ribbon on each end of title strip; attach with red brad on left. Set silver eyelet in heart sticker; attach to title bar on right. Double mat photo on purple and black cardstocks; mount on page. Mat words printed on purple cardstock with black cardstock. Punch hole in one journaling block; hang heart charm from beaded chain. Adhere matted words on photo and page with foam adhesive.

Sharon Whitehead, Vernon, British Columbia, Canada

Supplies: Blue, purple and black textured cardstocks (Bazzill); heart sticker (EK Success); gingham ribbon; red brad; silver brad; key chain; heart charm

Anne Marley

Design a page with cultural distinction

Honor cultural heritage with a distinctive page design that incorporates decorative accents. Begin with a purple cardstock background. Stamp corner design onto page; heat emboss in gold. Wrap piece of cardstock with floral fabric; mat on light purple cardstock. Sew fabric to mat along edges with purple floss; affix to background page. Triple mat photo on purple mulberry papers and adhere to page. Print journaling captions on purple mulberry; tear out and affix on page. Embellish captions with strung beads. Cut section from purple foam with decorative scissors. Stamp image onto foam and emboss with gold embossing powder; adhere to page. Finish page by accenting with decorative gold fan and flower charms.

Andrea Lyn Vetten-Marley, Aurora, Colorado

Supplies: Craft foam (Darice); floral fabric (VIP Cranston Prints); purple mulberry papers (Westrim); corner stamp (Inkadinkado); word stamp (PSX Design); decorative corners (Jesse James); gold fan charm (Magic Scraps); gold embossing powder; purple cardstocks; embossing ink; purple floss

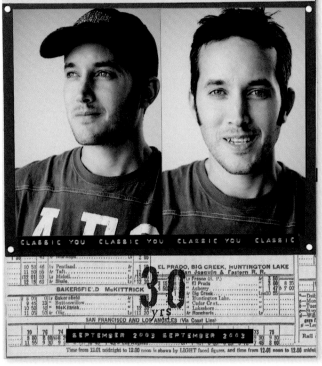

Supplies: Patterned paper (Rusty Pickle); label (Dymo); letter and number stamps (PSX Design, Ma Vinci's); letter stickers (Creative Imaginations); slide mounts (Impress Rubber Stamps); moss and black cardstocks; white brads; black ink

Classic Victor

Showcase a sibling

Feature a sibling center stage with striking black-and-white photos and a clean design. Begin with two moss-colored cardstock backgrounds. For left page, print title directly onto top of background. Cut section of patterned paper; adhere along bottom. Stamp age on paper with various number and letter stamps. Mat photos on black cardstock and adhere on left page with white brads. Affix labels on bottom of page and beneath photos. For right page, journal on bottom of background. Print "THE" on section of patterned paper; adhere on top of page. Affix label along edge of patterned paper. Mat photo on black cardstock; mount on page. Use label and letter stickers to apply caption on patterned paper. Adhere black slide mounts over stickers and cut frame from black cardstock; mount over "THE" with white brads.

Joy Bohon, Bedford, Indiana

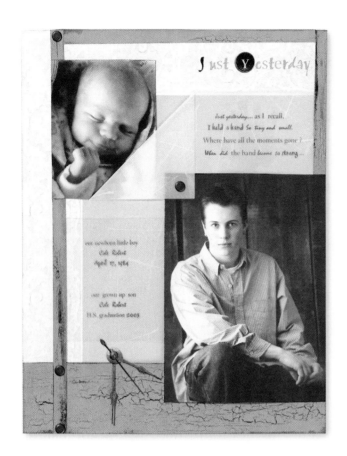

Just Yesterday

Reflect on the passing of time

Use a folded corner to reveal a photo from the past and to direct the eye to a photo in the present. Begin by printing title onto a patterned paper background; heat emboss "J" with clear embossing powder to enhance. Apply letter sticker over "Y." For crackle borders, paint colored cardstock randomly with black acrylic paint; apply crackle medium and green paint, allowing for dry time between each. Lightly sand; cut out and layer on page with green patterned paper, attaching snaps on thin border strip. Mount baby photo on page. Print poem on patterned vellum; layer on background page with current photo. Fold corner to reveal baby photo; attach with snap. Print dates on transparency; sprinkle with clear embossing powder and heat to set. Cut out and adhere on page. Add clock hands to finish.

Linda Albrecht, St. Peter, Minnesota
Photo: Shaydes Of Color, New Ulm, Minnesota

Supplies: Patterned paper (Anna Griffin, It Takes Two); letter sticker (EK Success); black and green paints (Delta); crackle medium (Plaid); antique snaps (Making Memories); patterned vellum (It Takes Two); clock hand (Walnut Hollow); clear embossing powder; kraft cardstock; transparency

My Sisters

Feature unique paper folding

Make a striking sister page that features beautiful paper folding and a glimpse into the past with an old photo. Begin with a green patterned paper background. Adhere section of green cardstock for border. Create triple-matted paper frames to house metal plaques from green cardstock, white patterned paper and sienna cardstock; adhere. Craft peekaboo opening from double-sided patterned paper by cutting slits into center of squares to form four triangles. Affix metal plaques inside; pull back triangles and attach to frames with green brads. Triple mat focal photo on green and sienna cardstocks and patterned paper; cut opposite corners from bottom two mats and adhere on page. Mat old photo on green cardstock; affix over section cut from patterned paper matted on green cardstock. Cut opposite corners from green mat. Make peekaboo frame from vellum piece; roll back openings and adhere over patterned paper mat, revealing photo. Attach swirl clips. Journal on vellum; cut out and adhere next to photo. Apply title with page pebble letters mounted on patterned paper and small silver frames tied with silver thread.

Arlene Santos, Mililani, Hawaii

Supplies: Patterned paper (Creative Imaginations, Die Cuts With A View); metal plaques, page pebbles, metal swirl clips (Making Memories); silver frames (source unknown); sienna and green cardstocks; green brads; silver thread

Sister...I loved being a sister as a child...when we got along. There is no greater champion than an older brother and I truly believe that every little girl should have one; and every little girl should have a baby brother to dress up like a doll (or at least in matching outfits!) This relationship is perhaps one of the most difficult to reconcile as an adult; The hierarchy of childhood is gone, and in it's place, grown beings of a common bond; not always with a common mindset. I love both my brothers and sister deeply, and continue to work toward a greater appreciation of the adults we have all become. It is my one of my greatest hopes that my own children value their sibling relationship and continue to grow in love throughout their lives.

When I think of when I nearly lost you... and now to have you back, so whole (and with a child of your own!) My heart fills daily with Gratitude

*And I've gotten some pretty great nieces and nephews out of them, too!

Sister...

Create a computer-generated page

Having siblings is a special gift. Creating a layout that pays tribute to how they enrich your life is a meaningful gesture to express your good fortune. This computer-generated page was created using Photoshop Elements 2. Begin by scanning and cropping a photo; reduce the opacity to 50 percent. Copy photo onto the work area and resize the scale to fit the page background. Create initial at bottom right corner. Apply all text passages. Scan twine and apply bevel and drop shadow; place across top of page. Scan swirl clips and additional photos, applying sepia tint to one. "Hang" colored photos from swirl clips and twine. Place larger photo at bottom left corner; apply shadow to all photos to complete. To manually re-create this page, enlarge a photo to fit page background; print onto vellum. Cut initial from green paper with a craft knife and affix over right corner. Print journaling onto a transparency; layer captions where desired. String twine across top of page, adhering in back. Mat sepia-tinted photo and attach remaining two photos to twine with swirl clips and adhesive. Mount entire page on white cardstock to complete.

Megan Stiles, Bend, Oregon

Brothers & Sisters

Create pull-out cards

Recall your fondest memories of childhood with informative pull-out cards written by you and your siblings. Begin by matting textured green cardstock on a textured brown cardstock background. Adhere enlarged photo on page. Stamp various dragonfly images on neutral cardstock; cut out, adhere on page and layer with vellum quote. Treat library card envelopes with olive ink; mount on page. Stamp names onto envelopes with moss ink. Print individual photos on vellum; cut out and double mat on brown and neutral-colored cardstocks. Print each individuals' fondest memories of childhood onto vellum squares; cut out and mount below respective photos. Laminate each card and slip into coordinating envelope. Print title on neutral cardstock. Adhere over focal photo beneath silver label holder attached with fiber; wrap around page and secure on back with tape. Embellish upper corner with preprinted ribbon, oval copper plate and raised stickers adhered atop plate.

Janetta Abucejo Wieneke, Memory Makers Books

Supplies: Textured cardstocks (Bazzill); dragonfly stamps (Stampabilities, Stampendous, Rubber Stampede); vellum quote (Memories Complete); library card envelopes (Anima Designs); letter stamps (Hero Arts); silver label holder (Magic Scraps); preprinted ribbon (7 Gypsies); oval plate (Li'l Davis Designs); raised stickers (K & Company); neutral cardstock; moss and olive inks; vellum; fiber; tape

Brothers & Sisters

the happiest moments of my life
have been the few
I have passed at home
in the bosom
of my family.
—Thomas Jefferson

Estes Park

Supplies: Patterned paper; green and sienna cardstocks; vellum; chalk; fiber; tag frames; silver brads; copper wire mesh; metal letters; fibers; metal stamps

Record the events of a family vacation

Embarking on an outdoor adventure with your family members is a memory you won't want to forget. Begin with two green cardstock background pages. Adhere photos on left page. Tear section of sienna cardstock; cut openings for photos and mount on page. String green fiber around silver brads over bottoms of three photos. Use metal letter stamps to impress words on sienna cardstock; accent with silver brad. Print definition on patterned papers; cut out and adhere. Stamp quote on upper left corner of page with letter stamps and brown ink. Print author name on vellum; tear out, chalk slightly in sienna, and staple below quote. Wrap fiber around tag frame; adhere on page. Affix copper wire mesh on bottom of page; cover with tag frames and add metal letters for title. Stamp date into background with metal stamps. For right page, adhere photos; cover with torn and cut sienna cardstock to reveal photos beneath. String fiber across top photo with silver brads. Print definitions and journaling on patterned paper; cut out and adhere on page. Stamp words on sienna cardstock piece; adorn with mesh, tag frame and brad to finish.

Natalie Abbott, Lakewood, Colorado

Mom & Me

Create a collage border

Piece together an interesting border with a collection of nostalgic stickers, buttons and charms to complement an enlarged photo. Begin with a burgundy cardstock background. Tear left edge of tan cardstock section; chalk edges in green and layer on page with striped patterned paper. Mount enlarged photo on background. Journal on vellum; cut out and adhere on page. Create collage border with various stickers, buttons, charms and burgundy velvet ribbon.

Misty Posey, Decatur, Alabama

Supplies: Patterned paper (Creative Imaginations); stickers (EK Success); charms and clock face (7 Gypsies); burgundy and tan cardstocks; vellum; buttons; red velvet ribbon

The Love Of Our Father...

Craft a symbolic collage

Create a collage with elements that hold symbolic meaning and are beautiful as well. Begin with a script patterned paper background; layer torn sections of various patterned papers on page. Ink torn edges of papers in dark red; roll edges. Add hand stitched "X" pattern along edge of one torn layer. Double mat photo on black cardstock and patterned paper; roll and ink corners of paper and adhere on page. Affix ruler sticker, tucking end under layer. Apply part of title with letter stamps onto cloth swatch and crumpled tag; add heart stamp on cloth. Adhere tag to page center; add buttons and mount onto page. Wrap yarn around buttons. Stick pin through cloth title and mount on page. Adhere remainder of title with letter tiles and letter stamps on ruler sticker. Mount label holder over cloth title with brads. Tear heart from patterned paper; ink edges in red, roll slightly and adhere on page, stitching two rows of thread across width. Finish page with date on bottom and flower cut-out on top corner.

Candi Gershon, Fishers, Indiana

Supplies: Patterned papers, flower cut out, ruler and date stickers (K & Company); letter stamps (PSX Design); label holder (Making Memories); letter tiles (Westrim); buttons, brads; tag; cloth; red and black inks; floss

Supplies: Patterned paper (Autumn Leaves); textured mustard cardstock (Bazzill); rub-on word, metal word eyelet (Making Memories); dog tag (Chronicle Books); silver eyelet; vellum; tag; fibers; metal-rimmed tag

Laughter

Catch a characteristic on film

Capture some playful moments between a sibling and your camera for a page with a fun, spontaneous feel. Begin by adhering torn strip of textured mustard cardstock on right edge of patterned paper. Machine stitch along straight edges. Mat two photos on black cardstock; set silver eyelet in bottom of top photo. Hang dog tag with jute; adhere all photos on page. Journal on vellum; cut out and mount on mustard border. Set pair of eyelets and knotted jute at top of vellum block and at bottom of mustard border. Apply title with rub-on. For tag accent, mat torn patterned paper on mustard cardstock; machine stitch onto aged tag. Adhere metal-rimmed tag, tied fiber and printed vellum strip on tag; adhere to page with eyelet word.

Cindy Johnson, Allen, Texas

The letter in the frame reads:

Dear Sister,

Here we are again. Another birthday, another inevitable step forward into the midst of life. This year, we'll both be in the same decade again, this dreaded period of mid-life crises and existential questions. So how are we doing? What have we achieved so far? I think we've done alright and fared pretty well. We might be a little rough around the edges, a little frayed and worn at times, and we are no longer size 8 or even 10. But we have loving partners, our kids are beautiful and successful, and we are mostly happy. I only wish we could live closer to each other, so we could affect each other's lives more directly. Who knows what will happen this decade, though? All I know is that you've aged with style and grace, and that I'm happy for your success. As they say, it's all downhill from here, and that's actually a good thing... These are the fabulous forties, and we're ready.

Supplies: Patterned papers (Creative Imaginations); pewter heart (Magenta); letter and charm stickers (Creative Imaginations, EK Success); clock charm (www.scrapsahoy.com); frame (My Mind's Eye); vellum; brass oval frame (Nunn Design); cream cardstock; brown and black inks; fabric; antique brads; ribbon; buttons

Fabulous Forties

Combine French country with shabby chic

Incorporate two distinctive styles for an eye-pleasing spread celebrating a special birthday. Begin with two cream cardstock background pages. Layer torn sections from various patterned papers on both backgrounds. Create photo mat for left page from torn blue patterned paper; treat edges with brown ink. Mount photo and adhere. Cut vellum frame for photo by crumpling and altering with brown ink. Attach frame over photo with brads; ink pewter heart with black ink and adhere at corner. Apply title with various letter stickers to fabric swatch, background page and torn and inked paper. Embellish with blue ribbon, clock charm and buttons. For right page, apply decorative stickers along torn edge; poke holes in centers and thread fabric through, tucking behind layer. Mat photo on torn and inked blue patterned paper. Affix torn strip on left side of matted photo; wrap with printed ribbon and adhere on page. Affix frame over photo. Journal on vellum; cut out, ink edges in brown and mount on photo. Embellish with small photo mounted in brass oval frame tied with blue ribbon.

Ann-Marie Weis, Oakland, California

Supplies: Heart charm (Welkmart); black and white cardstocks; die-cut letters (source unknown)

My Mother

Incorporate black and white for contrast

Clean lines, crisp design and the pleasing contrast of black and white makes for a striking layout. Journal and apply part of title directly onto white cardstock background using Broderbund software. Print second part of title onto cardstock; cut out, mount on black cardstock and adhere with foam adhesive. Die cut letters for the remainder of title from black cardstock. Mount photo on page. Hang heart charm from "V" with jump ring and adhere die-cut letters to page, mounting the "O" and "E" with foam adhesive. Cut strips and flowers from black cardstock; adhere strips around title, in center with flower and along edges of photo.

Sharon Whitehead, Vernon, British Columbia, Canada

Nanay Sweet As A Rose

Pay tribute to your mom

Moms hold a place in our hearts that deserve a very special page of their own. Begin with a black cardstock background. Create decorative corners with a corner punch. Layer background with rose-colored cardstock. Cut two sections of pink cardstock; tear along one edge and mount to top and bottom of page, tucking under decorative punched corners. Print focal photo with white border; adhere on page. Cut out rose image from ephemera book; affix on bottom of page. Print remaining black-and-white photo; colorize roses with pink photo-tinting markers. Journal on cloud vellum; cut out and mount on page. Apply title with letter stickers on top of page and on rose image at bottom. Finish by adorning photo with silk flower bunch at top corner.

Janetta Abucejo Wieneke, Memory Makers Books

Supplies: Corner punch (EK Success); rose image (Design Originals); photo tinting markers (Marshall's); cloud vellum (DMD); letter stickers (Wordsworth); black and pink cardstocks; silk flowers

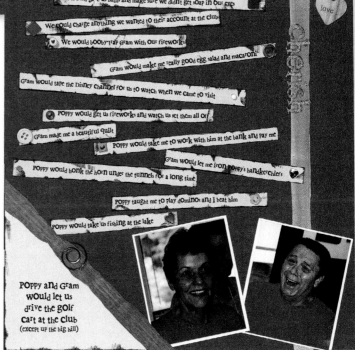

Poppy And Gram

Recall fond memories on journaling strips

Incorporate journaling strips that capture some of the wonderful memories created with your grandparents while you were a child. Begin with two red cardstock background pages. Print title and caption on opposite corners of textured pink cardstock; cut out, treat edges with black ink and affix on top corner of left page and bottom corner of right page. For left page, bend over upper left corner of background; attach inked pink cardstock piece on back of page and secure folded edge with heart mesh eyelet. Double mat photo on white and pink cardstocks; embellish bottom corner with pink buttons and layer on page with paint chip and border sticker. Chalk oval tag in red; tie off with gingham ribbon, apply letter sticker and mount on corner of matted photo. Apply rub-on word to sticker border; coat in diamond glaze and cover with tiny glass beads. Add poem stone and word sticker to finish page. For right page, apply border sticker vertically on page and apply rub-on word; cover in diamond glaze and beads. Journal on pink cardstock; cut into strips, ink in black and attach to page with various brads, eyelets, buttons and beads. Mat photos on white cardstock; mount on page. Add poem stone at top corner. Run pink spring roll paper across edge of pink cardstock corner pieces on both pages; attach swirl clips.

Lindsay Teague, Phoenix, Arizona

Supplies: Textured pink cardstock (Bazzill); border stickers, letter sticker, word sticker and poem stones (Creative Imaginations); rub-on words, heart mesh eyelets, swirl clips (Making Memories); crystal lacquer (JudiKins); pink spring roll paper (Magic Scraps); red, white and pink cardstocks; black ink; buttons; paint chip; red chalk; gingham ribbon; tiny glass beads; brads; beads; eyelets

Chapter Four

FRIENDS

I was always told that we never make friends as adults like we did in high school. But I don't believe that for one minute! Last year, I met Polly McMillan on the internet. We had both entered a scrapbooking contest & just had to share our layouts with someone..... ANYONE! The more we chatted, the more we found we had a lot in common. It felt as though we had known each other forever. Now we talk on the phone at least 3 times a week if not more. When things go rough in our lives, we can always call each other for comfort. I don't know what I'd do without her cheery voice. The most amazing part is that she came all the way from Arizona to Tennessee last year just to meet me. She's a true friend and one I wouldn't trade for ANYTHING in the world, not even a million scrapbook layouts published!
-2003

laugh ...... listen .... Love

You've Gotta Have Friends □

They're the ones who really know us and like us nonetheless. The ones we call for a favor, a shoulder, a cup of sugar or a word of advice. They'll let us know when our heads are big and our minds are small, when we've never been more brilliant or couldn't be more wrong. Motivational cheerleaders to champion our greatest victories and steadfast confidants in our moments of defeat, friends are the second families and first mates that navigate us through life. Whether they're friends from schoolyard days or ones found later in life, recognizing our friendships in scrapbook pages is as unique an expression of gratitude as each one-of-a-kind relationship shared. Not to be forgotten, our furry, four-legged companions have earned a place all their own in our albums for the camaraderie they unconditionally provide. Friendship, in all its forms and contexts, is ready inspiration and cause for celebration in scrapbook pages.

Supplies: Brown handmade paper (Club Scrap); patterned papers (7 Gypsies, K & Company); copper embossing powder (PSX Design); metal word, page pebble (Making Memories); tag template (Deluxe Designs); red and cream cardstocks; chalk; circle and heart brads; eyelets; fibers

Priceless

Dedicate a page in someone's memory

Honor the memory of a passed loved one with personal journaling inside photo cards. Begin with two 8 x 8" brown handmade paper backgrounds. Cut sections from patterned paper and mount onto each page; heat emboss edges in copper. On left page, mat photo on red cardstock; adhere onto blank card. Emboss card edges in copper; journal inside and mount on page. Print poem on cream cardstock; cut out, chalk edges and mount on torn brown cardstock mat. Adhere onto page. Finish page with copper embossed heart brad and metal title word. On right page, adhere photo onto card; mat on red patterned paper and mount on page. Use template to create tag; set eyelet, embellish with crumpled cardstock heart, button and fibers. Finish page with embossed brads and page pebble over name at bottom corner.

Colleen Chase, Streamwood, Illinois

Friends

Symbolize individuality with mixed patterns

Friends can remain close even when life takes them down separate paths. Showcase that in a layout that combines different but harmonious patterns. Begin by journaling onto a brown cardstock background page; treat edges with black ink. Adhere various square sections of sanded patterned papers onto bottom of page; layer with strip of textured black cardstock. Stamp date on textured white cardstock; affix beneath label holder with copper brads on border strip. Create border along top of page with strips of black textured cardstock and floral patterned paper. Mat bottom photo on white textured cardstock; mount on page. Mount top photo on page beneath red faux wood frame. Print title on black textured cardstock; cut with a craft knife and adhere on page, dotting "i" with a button.

Jennifer Bourgeault, Macomb Township, Michigan

Supplies: Patterned paper, red faux wood frame (Daisy D's); textured black and white cardstocks (Bazzill); date stamp, label holder (Making Memories); brown cardstock; black ink; copper brads; button

Ben

Sum up a friend's special qualities

Honor a friendship in a page by documenting your shared interests and the characteristics you admire about your friend. Begin with a patterned paper background. Layer torn sections of patterned paper and brown cardstock to create a border along left side. Print qualities and commonalities on tan cardstock; cut out and mount on page, tucking phrases into border. Affix letter stickers randomly on page. Double mat photo on patterned paper and brown cardstock; adhere to page. Apply title with letter stickers. Embellish formica tags with scraps of paper, mini scrapbook tiles and mica flakes; seal with dimensional adhesive and outline with gold leafing pen. Affix tags on corrugated scrap strip with gold brads. Wrap gold thread around corrugated strip; adhere onto border.

Mendy Douglass, Frankfort, Kentucky

Supplies: Patterned papers (Wordsworth, 7 Gypsies); letter stickers (EK Success, Wordsworth); formica tags (Lowe's); mini wooden letter tiles (Limited Edition Rubberstamps); mica flakes (USArtQuest); dimensional adhesive (JudiKins); gold leafing pen (Krylon); brown cardstock; gold brads; scrap corrugated cardboard

Best Of Friends

Create a masculine layout

Use browns to accentuate a black-and-white photo of best friends for a masculine look. Trim textured brown cardstock and treat edges with black ink; mount on textured dark brown cardstock background. Adhere inked section of patterned paper across page. Mat photo on textured tan cardstock; treat edges with black ink and adhere onto page. Affix gingham ribbon across bottom of page. Adorn with letter stickers; frame with large silver conchos. Apply letter stickers for title; add tag and number stickers for date on page to finish.

Elizabeth Cuzzacrea, Lockport, New York

Supplies: Textured brown cardstocks (Bazzill); patterned paper (DMD); title letter stickers, tag and number stickers (EK Success); large silver conchos (Scrapworks); black ink; gingham ribbon

David and Thunder

Capture a moment between companions

Remember to appreciate each moment—including the quiet ones in the company of a furry friend. Begin with a patterned paper background. Tear two sections of striped patterned paper; treat edges with black ink and layer on background page. Mat photo on white cardstock; mount on page. Tie white ribbon around bottom of page; stamp with letter stamps. Stamp title and date onto white cardstock; cut out and mat on back of patterned paper mat. Cut at corners, fold edges over and machine stitch onto cardstock; punch holes at top and string ribbon through. Adhere with foam adhesive onto page.

Laura Stewart, Fort Wayne, Indiana

Supplies: Patterned papers (KI Memories); letter stamps (Hero Arts); number stamps (PSX Design); white cardstock; white ribbon; black ink

Friends

Mix bold patterns

Capture the fun and spunky spirit of your friendship by mixing bold patterns. Begin by matting patterned paper on a red cardstock background; layer on page with torn section of patterned paper. Accent edge of torn paper with metal flower charm tied to gingham ribbon. Mat photo on red cardstock; mount on page. Journal on red cardstock, leaving room at top for title. Wrap gingham ribbon around journal box; layer with metal word. Tear bottom off journaling box, roll slightly and adhere to page. Attach small photo on underside of metal-rimmed tag; tie off with cardstock strip and mount beneath photo.

Shawni Reynolds, Santee, California

Supplies: Patterned papers (Paper Fever, 7 Gypsies); metal charm, metal word, metal-rimmed tag (Making Memories); red cardstock; gingham ribbon

Jac, Leah, Beth, Sarah

Create an abstract title

Craft an eye-catching title by forming letters from the negative space created by arranging cut pieces of cardstock. Begin with a tan cardstock background page. Journal onto orange cardstock; cut out, treat with brown chalk and adhere with cropped photos onto page. Use a color-blocking technique to cut various colored textured and un-textured cardstock pieces to form letters when adhered to background; chalk in brown and mount on page.

Leah Blanco Williams, Kansas City, Missouri

Supplies: Tan, yellow, orange, green, blue, purple and pink cardstocks; brown chalk

Friendships

Cut and connect bold shapes

Cut graphic shapes with a craft knife and link them together for visual interest. Begin with a black cardstock background. Trim edges of black cardstock background with red cardstock strips. Mat photo on red cardstock. Print journaling onto textured white cardstock; cut out and mat on red cardstock, leaving room for matted photo. Layer all onto page. Print title onto white cardstock; cut out with craft knife and affix on page, double matting three letters on white and red cardstocks. For square accents, punch and cut various squares and square frames from red and white cardstocks; mat white squares on red cardstock. Embellish with square gold brads and mount all on page using foam adhesive where desired.

Sharon Whitehead, Vernon, British Columbia, Canada

Supplies: Textured white cardstock (Bazzill); white, red and black cardstocks; square gold brads; craft knife; foam adhesive

A Boy And His Dog

Celebrate furry companions

Dogs hold a very special place in human hearts and deserve a page all their own! Begin with a textured brown cardstock background. Layer sections cut from patterned papers on page; adhere photo at top corner. Journal onto textured green cardstock; cut out, mat on light green cardstock and adhere on page. Create title by printing some words on blue and green cardstocks; mat on tan and green cardstocks and adhere on page. Finish title with letter sticker and label. Print caption on green cardstock; punch into circle, set black eyelet and string around bottom of page with green floss. Adhere black slide frame over cropped photo on bottom corner; embellish with sewn brown button.

Melissa Predmore, Aloha, Oregon

Supplies: Brown, tan, blue and green textured cardstocks (Bazzill); patterned papers (KI Memories); label maker (Dymo); letter sticker (Creative Memories); black slide mount; green floss; black eyelet; brown button

Dare To Play

Incorporate several textures

Combine several subtle textures for an appealing page design. Begin with a textured brown cardstock background. Layer photo on background page over torn textured dark green and light green cardstock sections, mesh and coastal netting. Accent page with definitions that have been altered with brown chalk. Embellish cardstock and mesh with copper brads, "hanging" copper plate from one with fiber. Adhere plate to page to secure. Apply rub-on words to photo and green cardstock section; write date along the side to complete.

Michaela Young-Mitchell, Morenci, Arizona

Supplies: Textured brown, dark green and light green cardstocks (Bazzill); maruyama mesh (Magenta); costal netting (Magic Scraps); definition stickers, rub-on words (Making Memories); copper tag (www.twopeasinabucket.com); brown chalk; copper brads; fibers

Boo-Bah

Honor your four-legged friends

Include the endearing term you call your faithful companions on a page that celebrates the special friendship they provide. Begin by trimming and matting patterned paper on textured gray cardstock; adhere strips cut from textured gray cardstock across page. Mount all photos. Attach eyelet phrases below two photos. Journal on vellum; cut out and mount on bottom left corner and adorn with dog paw print stickers. Mat letter stickers on gray cardstock; affix on upper right corner of page. Stamp dogs and dog bowl on vellum with watermark ink; cover with embossing puff powder and heat to set. Cut out and adhere below title with foam adhesive. Stamp dogs' names with letter stamps and teal and blue inks; sprinkle with clear embossing powder and heat to set. Punch out letters with circle punch and affix on page with foam adhesive.

Janetta Abucejo Wieneke, Memory Makers Books

Supplies: Patterned paper, letter stickers for title (American Crafts); textured cardstock (Bazzill); eyelet phrases (Making Memories); paw print stickers (EK Success); dog stamp (All Night Media); dog dish stamp (Stamps By Judith); watermark ink (Tsukineko); typewriter key letter stamps (Prickly Pear); embossing puff powder, clear embossing powder; vellum; teal and blue inks

Supplies: Patterned papers, letter stickers, and tag (Chatterbox); date stamp (Making Memories); letter stamp (PSX Design); black ink; taupe and blue cardstocks; cheesecloth; brads; twine

Friends By Chance

Showcase a special friendship

A long-distance friendship is special because it withstands the separation. Make a special layout featuring that faraway friend. Begin by sanding edges of a taupe cardstock background page. Apply letter stickers for title onto sanded tan patterned paper strip; layer on page with cheesecloth and sanded blue patterned paper section. Attach to page with blue brads to form title bar. Journal on tan patterned paper; cut out, sand edges and layer onto page with sanded blue patterned paper, attaching with blue and tan brads. Mat both photos on blue cardstock; stamp date on corners of each photo. Mount photos on page, using foam spacers for secondary photo. Stamp names on tag; tie off with twine and layer on page with cheesecloth, wrapping twine around back of page to secure.

Trudy Sigurdson, Victoria, British Columbia, Canada

I Believe In Angels

Honor a special "earth angel"

Pay tribute to a favorite person by creating a reflective page in his or her honor. Begin with two patterned paper backgrounds. For left page, create title strip by layering torn green cardstock section on red cardstock strip. Heat emboss edges in silver; embellish with fiber and mesh and affix on page. Attach "Believe" sticker; apply remainder of title with letter stickers and letters stamped on metal pieces. Embellish with charms, buttons and safety pin. Create photo mat by inking torn edges of green and red cardstock sections; layer and machine stitch to page. Layer with photo, mesh, feather and caption. Journal on transparency and adhere over photo with silver brad. Print excerpt from song onto transparency; adhere on page. Cut square from patterned paper; adhere below cut-out "grace" strip. On right page, repeat photo mat technique; layer with photo, fiber and caption printed on transparency. For border, layer white mesh over a green cardstock strip; adhere vertically on page. Attach pre-made framed angels. Journal on green cardstock; cut into strips and slip into envelope wrapped in mesh and embellished with charm. Adhere on page. Journal onto green cardstock; tear and adhere over mesh on page. Embellish corner with cut square from patterned paper, feathers and charm.

Ursula Riley, Madison, Alabama

Supplies: Patterned papers (Club Scrap); mesh (Magic Mesh); letter stickers (EK Success); letter stamps (Inkadinkado); envelope (Foofala); green and red cardstocks; assorted charms; transparency; safety pin; black and green inks; premade framed angels; buttons

Supplies: Textured light green cardstock (Bazzill); patterned papers (Chatterbox); letter stickers (Creative Imaginations); letter stamps (PSX Design); page pebbles, silver frame and ribbon charm (Making Memories); black ink

Karen My Cosmic Twin

Display your favorite photos

Show off your favorite photos of you and a good friend while at the same time telling the story of how you met. Begin with a textured light green cardstock background for left page and mauve patterned paper for the right page. Journal directly onto left page. Adhere section of mauve patterned paper along bottom of page; apply title to border with letter stamps, page pebbles and letter stickers. Crop photo and layer beneath silver frame; mount on bottom of left page. Slide ribbon charm through strip of patterned paper; affix on top of page. For right page, print photos in black-and-white. Crop photos and various patterned papers into equal-sized squares; mount on patterned paper background in checkerboard fashion.

Jennifer Miller, Humble, Texas

Supplies: Patterned paper (Two Busy Moms); patterned vellum (Treehouse Designs); printed twill ribbon, wire holder (7 Gypsies); stamps (Hero Arts); staples, metal and metal stamp kit (Making Memories); black and red cardstocks; mustard and khaki papers; domino; photo corners

Sonia's Birthday

Mix bold colors and patterns

Combine several patterns and page elements for an eye-pleasing party page. Begin with two black card-stock background pages. For left page, journal and stamp onto khaki strip; mount vertically. Affix printed twill ribbon across page with red staples; layer with stamped domino. Mount patterned vellum section across top of page. Create mosaic accent from black cardstock mounted on mustard paper; cut sections from patterned paper and adhere. Single and double mat photos on khaki and patterned papers and mustard cardstock; ink edges of mustard mat with black ink. Conjoin photos with wire holder and adhere to page. Create card from red cardstock. Decorate cover with mustard cardstock, defini-tion sticker, raffia and gold snaps; mount to background page. For right page, cut section from patterned paper; mount along left side. Mat two photos on mustard and khaki papers; accent one photo with photo corners. Attach printed twill ribbon across page with red staples; adhere photos. Layer corner of border strip with corner torn from patterned vellum. Accent bottom photo with stamped strip of torn vellum, metal-stamped metal scrap and staples. Complete page with tag adorned with patterned paper sections, heart, brads and hemp.

Shan Blake, Aliso Viejo, California

GUYS WITH EARRINGS

Take two adult males, add middle-aged mentality, restless spirits and a current fashion trend, and what do you get? Guys with earrings!

From the time his son Greg exercised his 18-year old freedom by returning from the state tourney in Madison with earrings, Jonathan Eastman decided he wanted holes in his head, too. Convincing Dick to join him in this adventure was less than easy, however. Finally, after church Jon gave him an ultimatum; pierce or not.

I, seeing a companion piece to my now-famous layout, wanted to come along to record the event. Jon told me no. "This isn't for girls. No girls allowed!"

They headed off to Claire's, and for all of Dick's hesitation, he went first. Both guys had chosen small gold studs, but when Jon's turn came, the woman said, "Oh my God!" Dick said at that moment, he wished he had brought his camera; Jon panicked and his face looked terrified, thinking he was dripping blood. No blood — she had placed a flashy diamond stud instead of the gold one!

A few days later, Dick was to meet Laverne Torgerson for coffee. Being retired, however had been gone for a few weeks. Dick was waiting with his head cupped over his left ear when Laverne arrived. He was shaking his head, and said, "For crying out loud, did you see what Jonathan went and did?" Dick smiled, put his hand down and replied, "It had company, Laverne!"

July 15, 2001

Guys With Earrings

Supplies: Letter stickers (Mrs. Grossman's); white, black and red cardstocks

Detail a spur-of-the-moment decision

Document an adventure your husband and a friend took that ended in a big surprise for you! Begin with two white background pages. Create filmstrip border for left page with cropped black-and-white photos matted on black cardstock section; separate center photo with red cardstock strips. Mount along side of left page. Apply title with letter stickers. Journal directly onto center of page. Embellish page with strips of black and red cardstocks. For right page, mat enlarged photo on large black cardstock mat. Affix strips of red cardstock across top and bottom of mat in alignment with cardstock strips on left page. Finish with strips of red and black cardstocks mounted on bottom of right page; add date beneath photo.

Gwyn Calvetti, West Salem, Wisconsin

The Best Laid Plans…

Document a grand plan gone awry

Getting several busy adults together is quite a task. It helps to look for the humor—and to create a fun layout—when the master plan falls apart. Begin with a black patterned paper background. Print story onto white cardstock; fold in half and stamp "pull" on one end. Print title onto green cardstock; cut into strip and envelope for journaling. Layer envelope, title and printed trip agenda onto page. Slide journaling into envelope. Embellish title strip with clock face cut from patterned paper and metal-rimmed tag frame.

Susan Cyrus, Broken Arrow, Oklahoma

Supplies: Patterned paper (KI Memories); letter stamps (Hero Arts); metal-rimmed tag frame (Making Memories); green cardstock; black ink; green envelope

The Girls Of Summer

Create depth with photo cropping

Put a unique cropping and layering technique to work to give an otherwise-ordinary photo an eye-catching, dimensional look. Form background page by layering blue mesh, beige mesh paper, ivory and blue cardstocks and corrugated paper on a brown cardstock background. To create dimensional photo, enlarge original and make four copies. Adhere one copy on page background. Using a craft knife, cut out people farthest in background. On copy three, cut out second row of people; on copy four, cut out foreground. Layer cut-outs onto copy adhered to page using foam adhesive. Cut frame from blue cardstock; affix with foam adhesive over dimensional photo. Embellish frame with stickers. Journal on vellum; cut out and adhere on page, rolling corners. Accent with dimensional stickers.

Julie Eickmeier, Fort Myers, Florida

Supplies: Corrugated paper (Current); blue mesh (Magic Mesh); brown mesh paper (Magenta); dimensional stickers (EK Success); stickers (source unknown); ivory, blue and brown cardstocks; vellum

Bosom Buddies

Tell the story of your friendship

Document how a special friendship developed and how it has endured over obstacles like distance and time. Begin with a patterned paper background. Double mat photo on ivory and brown patterned papers; mount on page. Journal on tan cardstock; cut out, mat on gray cardstock and adhere below photo. Affix duct tape word stickers along right side of page. Mount wooden frames at askew angles on top of mini photos along left side of page. Apply title on top of page with wooden letters.

Janetta Abucejo Wieneke, Memory Makers Books

Supplies: Patterned papers (Rusty Pickle); duct tape word stickers (Pebbles Inc.); wooden frames and letters (Li'l Davis Designs); tan and gray cardstocks

A Letter From Shep

Showcase a friend's letter

Scan and reduce a letter from a friend to incorporate into a page about your long-distance relationship. Begin with a blue cardstock backgound page. Print journaling onto tan cardstock; cut into a journaling block and individual caption strips. Scan, reduce and print letter. Mat letter, photo and journaling block on red cardstock. Accent each with journaling strips adhered with brass snaps; affix to page. Create title by applying letter stickers to tan cardstock block accented with snaps and circle; mount circle on red cardstock square with foam adhesive.

Janis Taylor, Miami, Florida

Supplies: Letter stickers (Creative Imaginations); brass snaps (Making Memories); blue, tan and red cardstocks

Kiss

Capture a pooch smooch

Create an endearing page about you and a beloved furry friend by allowing a precious photo to speak for itself. Begin by layering blue mesh paper and sections from two different patterned papers to a blue background page. Adhere piece of patterned paper on backside of upper right corner; fold over to expose striped paper and adhere over tag hanging from chain with rivet. Treat edges of tag with black ink; embellish with blue mesh, piece of torn corrugated cardstock, blue tied button and metal letters. Mount blue corrugated cardboard piece on back of page in upper right corner. Double mat photo on white cardstock and large torn blue corrugated mat; enhance corrugated mat with silver metallic rub-ons. Affix to page. Embellish mat with blue buttons tied with blue floss. Adhere label holder over "kiss" on patterned paper with brads. Stamp date on bottom left corner of page. Apply title on bottom of right corner with rub-on word.

Lindsay Teague, Phoenix, Arizona

Supplies: Blue mesh paper (Magenta); patterned papers (KI Memories, 7 Gypsies); chain (Anna & Bess); rivet (Chatterbox); metal letters, rub-on word, label holder, date stamp (Making Memories); silver metallic rub-ons (Craf-T); buttons; tag; brads

Two Peas In A Pod

Paint a faux wood frame and background

Showcase a special friendship photo by housing it inside a painted faux wood frame. Begin with a patterned paper background for left page and tan background paper for right page. Mount enlarged photo and adhere to left page. Paint rectangular section and pieces cut to form frame from cardboard with antique white acrylic paint; sand lightly to age. Wrap frame with raffia and mount atop photo on left page with brads. Mount rectangle section to right page. Tear corner sections from embossed green handmade paper; adhere on upper corner of left page and bottom corner of right page. Affix sanded floral tag on frame with rivets; tie raffia through and knot on left side. Mount vellum quote atop tag. Journal on patterned paper; tear out and affix on right page, adding stitching on edges. Mount remaining photos; layer top photo with memorabilia and floral sticker. Print names on vellum and mount on photo. Stamp date on patterned paper; cut out and affix on metal tag. Tie off tag with raffia and adhere to page.

Heather Melzer, Yorkville, Illinois

Supplies: Patterned papers, embossed green handmade paper (Anna Griffin); antique white acrylic paint (Delta); floral tag (Me & My Big Ideas); rivets (Chatterbox); vellum quotes (Memories Complete); floral sticker (EK Success); metal tag (Magic Scraps); date stamp (Office Max); tan paper; silver brads; raffia; cream floss

Old Friends

Feature the story behind
your friendship

Document how a special friendship that has stood the test of time developed with a layout that focuses on a single photo and journaling. Begin by mounting vertical sections of various patterned papers on a textured brown cardstock background. Wrap lace around bottom of page, securing on back. Print journaling on stitched specialty paper, leaving room for matted photo. Adhere on page with brads and gold bow charm. Mat photo on tan textured cardstock, leaving room at top for title; enhance edges with copper metallic rub-ons. Adhere lace on mat above photo, securing on back; mount on page. Adorn bottom corner with decorative photo corner. Apply title at top of mat with letter stickers and page pebbles. Embellish with brads and gold flower accent.

Gayle Hodgins, Philadelphia, Pennsylvania

Supplies: Textured brown and tan cardstocks (Bazzill); patterned papers (Hot Off The Press, Paper Company, 7 Gypsies); stitched specialty paper (Magic Scraps); gold charms and photo corner (Lifetime Moments); letter stickers (EK Success); page pebbles (Making Memories); copper metallic rub-ons (Craf-T); lace ribbon; brads

Supplies: Plum handmade paper (Club Scrap); gold embossing powder (Stampendous); swirl hearts, label holder (Making Memories); dimensional adhesive (JudiKins); plum, tan and green cardstocks; brads

Kristen & Sasha

Customize a background page

Pay tribute to the companionship found in a canine friend with customized patterned paper. Use Microsoft Word to repeat phrase and names; print on tan cardstock. Layer torn strip of handmade paper horizontally across page. Trim and machine stitch patterned paper and torn strip onto plum cardstock background; treat edges of background with dark blue ink. Cut cardstock corner pieces; heat emboss with several layers of gold embossing powder; set swirl heart in melted powder. Attach on right corners of page. Double mat right photo on light and dark green cardstocks; tear top and bottom edges off mat and mount on page, tucking bottom under handmade paper. Print quote and journaling on light green cardstock; detail with black pen and mat on dark green cardstock, tearing bottom edge off mat. Adhere on page, tucking top edge under handmade paper; adorn with gold embossed swirl heart. Emboss edge of journaling box; mount on page beneath photo. Create photo frame from light green cardstock; tear out center for opening and roll edges. Cut mat for photo from dark green cardstock; crumple, wet, flatten and squeeze edges. When dry, layer on page with frame and photo with gold embossed brads. Emboss label holder in gold; attach to page over date with green fibers; secure on back of page. Cut title from green cardstock with craft knife using computer font as a guide. Adhere on handmade paper and cover in dimensional adhesive.

Michelle Pendleton, Colorado Springs, Colorado

The Road To A Friend's Is Never Long

Feature a gift card from a friend

Incorporate a card given to you by a friend across the miles for a page that signifies that friendship knows no distance. Begin with a red cardstock background; adhere striped border stickers along top and bottom of page. Print caption on tan cardstock; tear out, crumple and ink. Layer with torn section of crumpled and inked patterned paper on page. Affix leaf stickers on crumpled paper sections and under acrylic circle and oval pieces; adhere circle on bottom of page. Tie several fibers through oval acrylic piece; mount along left side and secure fibers on back of page. Mount card with foam adhesive on top of page. Mat photos on tan cardstock; adhere on page.

Andrea Steed, Rochester, Minnesota

Supplies: Border and leaf stickers (Pebbles Inc.); patterned paper (7 Gypsies); acrylic pieces (Sunday International); red cardstock; dark brown ink; fibers

Palsy

Heat-stamp velvet

Stamp an image on velvet for an elegant look. Begin with a red velvet section, decorative stamp and iron set on highest setting. Lay stamp image-side-up on ironing board; lay velvet paper velvet-side-down on stamp and press with iron for 15-20 seconds. Lightly stamp image in black ink randomly on recently ironed velvet. Journal on tan cardstock background; embellish bottom corner with decorative tag tied with hemp cord and matted on tan cardstock. Die cut letters from tan cardstock; mount on tag. Adhere velvet section along top of page. Affix burlap ribbon, cropped photo matted on tan cardstock and tag aged with antique gold pigment paint; wrap around left edge of page and secure with eyelets. Tie hemp cord through eyelets in tag. Cut title from red velvet using lettering template; adhere over burlap ribbon.

Nancy Kort, Portland, Oregon
Photo: Amanda Anderson, Olympia, Washington

Supplies: Red velvet paper (Stampin' Up!); stamp (Club Scrap); shaped tags (Creative Imaginations); antique gold pigment paint (AMACO); Frankie die-cut letters (QuicKutz); lettering template (Wordsworth); tan cardstock; hemp cord; burlap ribbon; brads

Supplies: Patterned papers (Chatterbox, Memories Complete); title letter stickers (Wordsworth); gold embossing powder (All Night Media); phrase stickers (Bo-Bunny Press); dimensional word stickers (K & Company); cut-out accent (Memories Complete); word ribbon, square clips and definition sticker (Making Memories); rust, cardboard and dark red cardstocks; various-sized and shaped metal-rimmed tags; raffia; orange brads; various ribbons; chalk

True Friends

Alter metal-rimmed tags

Remove the centers from metal-rimmed tags to create the perfect frames for title letters. Begin by sanding edges of a rust background page; layer sanded and torn sections of patterned paper and kraft cardstock on background page. Create title border by layering patterned paper strip over dark red cardstock section; trim with ribbon and mount onto top of page, attaching with brads. Apply title with letter stickers. Remove centers from various-sized metal-rimmed tags; spot-emboss rims with gold embossing powder; tie raffia to each frame and adhere over individual letters. Affix dimensional word sticker on embellished title bar for first part of title. Mat photo on rust cardstock, leaving length at bottom for embellishing. Tear and roll back section in mat; cut small square from kraft cardstock; apply sticker phrase and adhere to backside of mat so that it is exposed under torn section. Embellish mat with dimensional word stickers and tag layered with torn paper and fence sticker. Print journaling on vellum; tear off bottom and adhere to page. Embellish with torn cardstock strip wrapped with raffia and tag embellished with cut-out accent. Chalk definition sticker and mount on bottom of page. Embellish page with layered torn strips of cardstock, ribbon, square clips and dimensional word stickers.

Kathy Fesmire, Athens, Tennessee

Andy

Slip notes inside a journaling pocket

Make a large journaling pocket to tuck notes of friendship into over time. Begin by tearing edges from patterned paper; line edges with black ink and adhere on a textured rust-colored cardstock background. Mat photos on torn black mulberry paper; adhere on page. Apply title with letter stickers on center of page. Embellish area around title with metal plaque and brads. Tear patterned vellum horizontally; ink torn edge in brown and attach across bottom of page with brads to form pocket. Print journaling onto clear vellum; tear out, ink edges in brown and attach to page with brads. Mat small photo on patterned paper; ink edges in brown and mount on pocket. Create large tag note card from patterned paper; ink edges in brown, apply letter stickers, punch hole and tie off with fibers. Slip into pocket.

Pam Canavan, Clermont, Florida

Supplies: Patterned paper, patterned vellum (Di Bona Designs); textured rust-colored cardstock (Bazzill); black mulberry (Pulsar); letter stickers (EK Success); metal plaque (Making Memories); black and brown inks; brads; fibers

Chapter Five

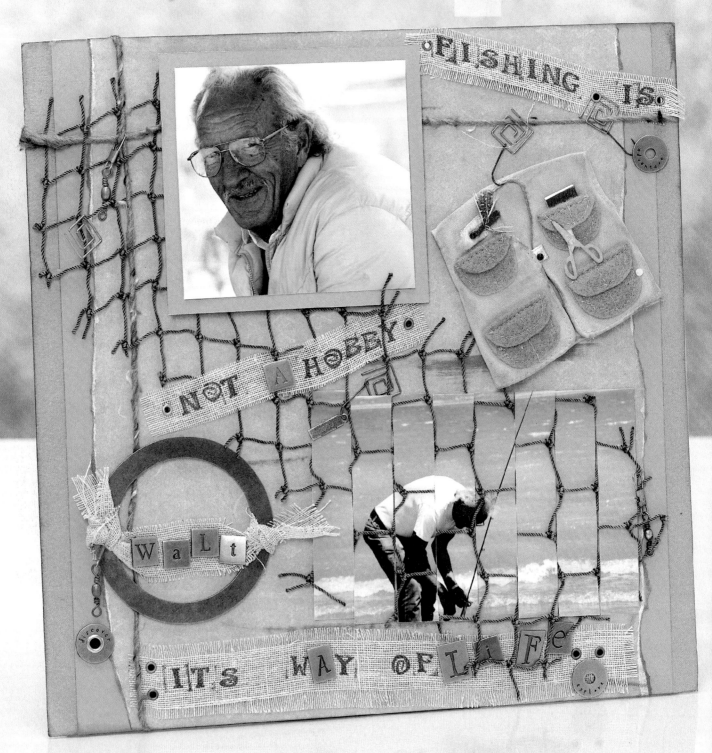

FISHING IS

NOT A HOBBY

WaLt

ITS WAY OF LIFE

Just For Fun □

When the day is done, the clock is punched, the sitter's been
called and the weekend is in sight, the hectic 9-to-5 grind comes to
a treasured temporary halt. In even the busiest of adult schedules
are priceless windows of opportunity to engage in recreational
pastimes and to pursue hobbies and around-the-house projects.
In scrapbooking our spare-time passions and activities, we not only
showcase our skills and talents in our pages, we produce tangible
evidence that grown-ups never outgrow fun. Adulthood invites all
kinds of good times—whether we cast our baited lines and patiently
await that fabled catch, tee off in anticipation of that coveted hole-
in-one, feel the wind on our faces on a full-throttle joy ride, or live
for a lively concert, playful game of poker or ambitious do-it-yourself
venture. When your grown-up responsibilities and obligations make
way for a moment of reprieve, record how you unwind in fun-
focused scrapbook pages.

Supplies: Patterned papers (Chatterbox); concho (Scrapworks); green cardstocks

Going Fishing?

Catch 'em telling a fish tale

Create a fun layout investigating a tale that seems a little "fishy" with photos and journaling that make a great case. Begin with green and olive cardstock background pages. On left page, print title on green background; cut out with craft knife. Adhere light green and olive cardstock sections to backside of page behind cut-out letters. Journal on light green cardstock; cut out and mount on pages. Layer various sections of patterned papers and various green cardstocks, continuing design across both pages. Affix small concho where border strips intersect on left page. Adhere photos to pages. Print captions for photos on right page on green cardstock; cut out and adhere on photos. Cut title letters from dark green cardstock with craft knife; adhere on pages, matting some words on green patterned paper. Finish by embellishing with various punched circles from various green cardstocks.

Jennifer Lessinger, Rockville, Minnesota

A Fish Story

Verify a catch with tape measure accents

Use tape measure stickers with masculine papers for a great layout featuring a successful fishing trip. Begin by lightly sanding brown paper for a page background. Tear burlap patterned paper; treat edges with black ink and mount on background page. Affix tape measure stickers vertically and horizontally along three sides of page. Sand vertical sticker; apply letter stickers. Mat photos on textured green cardstock and blue patterned paper mats; adhere on page. Apply "DAD" on bottom of upper photo with letter stickers. Create title with a variety of letter stickers and tag sticker across bottom of page. Print "summer" onto cream cardstock; cut out and mount on page under silver label holder sticker.

Linda Beeson, Ventura, California

Supplies: Patterned papers (Karen Foster Design); textured green cardstock (Bazzill); tape measure stickers, tag and dark label holder stickers (EK Success); letter stickers (Wordsworth, Me & My Big Ideas); silver label holder sticker (Sticker Studio); brown paper; sand paper; black ink

Golf

Feature a favorite passion

Use an enlarged photo to capture a moment spent engaged in a favorite pastime or hobby. Begin by mounting gingham ribbon on corners of green patterned paper background. Mat enlarged photo on vellum, leaving length on right side; fold over and punch holes at top and bottom. String plaid ribbon through and tie in bow; adhere on page. Use letter and number stamps to apply name and date on folded-over vellum. Stamp words above and below photo on background. Tear left edge of secondary photo and black cardstock mat; mount on page with foam adhesive. Stamp title on patterned paper; affix on page under decorative frame. "Hang" from plaid ribbon tied in a bow; adhere above frame.

Polly McMillan, Bullhead City, Arizona

Supplies: Patterned paper (Creative Imaginations, Scrap Ease); stamps (Hero Arts, PSX Design); decorative frame (Maude and Millie); gingham and plaid ribbons; black ink

A Friendly Game Of Golf

Go wild with your title

Build a mixed media and animal-print-adorned title bar for a page that walks a bit on the wild side. Adhere torn section of black cardstock vertically on brown cardstock background page; layer with crumpled and torn tan cardstock piece. Make "spears" from tan and gray cardstocks, twine and feathers; adhere on border. Cut "A" from animal print paper and black cardstock using die-cut machine; mount on top of border. Cut letters and circles from shrink plastic; zebra-stripe the letters and color the circles to resemble golf balls. Shrink according to package directions. Affix letter stickers on golf balls and adhere shrink elements on border with palm tree die cuts and black mesh. Create remainder of title with metal letters attached with black brads, letter beads mounted on vellum tag and pre-cut letters shadowed with black paper. Double mat on black cardstock and animal print paper. Stamp date on rust-colored paper; cut out and adhere bead border on back and black brads on ends. Attach to border with foam adhesive. Mat photos on rust-colored paper; adhere on page. Mat inked tag on brown paper mat; tie off with fibers, apply letter stickers and adhere on page. Freehand draw totem pole from various cardstocks; place on accordion-folded journal covered in mesh and animal print paper. Enhance design with various chalks. Journal inside. Create golf "putting green" with cardstock on last page. Mount brads on outside of book and on page; secure shut by wrapping twine around brads.

Kathy Fesmire, Athens, Tennessee

Supplies: Palm tree die cuts and letter "A" die cut (Sizzix); shrink plastic (Grafix); letter stickers (Wordsworth); pre-cut letters (Remember When); black mesh (Magic Mesh); animal print paper (Paper Company); metal letters, date stamp (Making Memories); bead trim (Style-a-bility); black, brown, tan, rust and green cardstocks; tag; black ink; black brads; fibers; chalk

A Little Alone Time

Record details from a special trip

Tell the story of a rare day alone together with a clean and simple layout. Begin with a light brown cardstock background. Print title onto textured green cardstock; cut out and mount across top of page. Adhere strip of textured black cardstock below title. Journal onto brown cardstock; cut out and affix on page along with focal photo. Layer strips of black, brown and green cardstock strips along bottom of page. Adhere cropped photo under silver frame to finish.

Nicole Cholet, Beaconsfield, Quebec, Canada

Supplies: Green and black textured cardstocks (Bazzill); silver frame (Making Memories); tan and brown cardstocks

A Moment Of Peace

Get inspired by nature

Echo the natural elements captured in an outdoors shot with earthy page additions. Treat the edges of a textured brown cardstock background page with black ink; layer sections of inked-edged patterned papers along top and bottom of page. Adhere copper photo corners on photo; mat on green patterned papers, inking edges in black. Mount on page. To create collage border embellishment, begin with brown textured cardstock piece inked in black; adhere over patterned paper section. Attach small image-embellished envelope with gold clip. Journal on patterned paper and slip inside envelope. Further accent cardstock with white mesh piece, corrugated piece, leather letter stickers, bottle tied with fiber, cut and chalked leaves, patterned papers, faux wax seal, clock face, clock numbers and bamboo piece. Apply title at top of page with leather letter stickers layered on page with leaves and corrugated pieces.

Vanessa Spady, Virginia Beach, Virginia

Supplies: Textured brown cardstock (Bazzill); patterned papers (Karen Foster Design); copper photo corners (Pioneer); gold clip (Treasured Memories); bamboo piece, clock numbers (Jest Charming); leather letter stickers (All My Memories); bottle, watch face (7 Gypsies); faux wax seal (Creative Imaginations); clock face and numbers

Come Out And Play

Show your silly side

Showcase a spontaneous and amusing photo that celebrates your silly side. Begin with a patterned paper background page. Enlarge and print photo with white border; detail edge with black pen and adhere on page. Affix purple ribbon across bottom of photo; adhere metal letters on ribbon. Print journaling on salmon vellum; cut out, detail edge in black and mount on bottom of page. Adhere buttons on photo paper; detail edges in black and mount on opposite corners of page. Apply rub-on word for title.

Trudy Sigurdson, Victoria, British Columbia, Canada
Photo: Leisa Cairns, Victoria, British Columbia, Canada

Supplies: Patterned paper (SEI); metal letters, rub-on words (Making Memories); glossy photo paper; vellum; buttons

Pool Shark

Record a passion

Create a bold billiards-themed page with striking photos and simple accents. Begin with a textured blue cardstock background page. Adhere red cardstock strips on center and bottom of page. Mount enlarged photos onto page. Cut diamonds from cardstock; heat emboss in pearl powder and mount on page. Journal and apply title on vellum; cut out and layer on page with remaining photo.

Susan Cyrus, Broken Arrow, Oklahoma

Supplies: Textured blue cardstock (Bazzill); watermark ink (Tsukineko); pearl embossing powder; red cardstock; vellum

A Fresh Perspective

Kick up your feet in a photo

Capture not only what you see in a photo, but how you see it for a fun page all about perspective. Begin with a textured blue cardstock background. Layer cut and torn sections of patterned papers along bottom of page. Apply title and date with letter and number stickers. Double mat photo on patterned papers; adhere on page, adorning corners with dimensional photo corners. Attach spiral on page with silver brad; string white fiber through spiral, twisting to resemble hammock and glue down on page. Attach bamboo clips. Journal on tag, tie off with fibers and mount over "hammock." Cut eyes from stamped images; color and mount along bottom of page.

Vanessa Spady, Virginia Beach, Virginia

Supplies: Textured blue cardstock (Bazzill); patterned paper, dimensional photo corners (K & Company); letter and number stickers (Colorbök); spiral (7 Gypsies); stamp (Magenta); bamboo clips (Jest Charming); silver brad; white fiber; tag; blue, brown, green and black pens

Supplies: Textured brown cardstock (Bazzill); patterned papers (Rusty Pickle, 7 Gypsies); white acrylic paint (DecoArt); silver rivets, silver square brads (Chatterbox); letter stickers (Creative Imaginations); brown and black inks

Wish

Construct a construction-themed layout

Document the construction of your dream house or a renovation project to show the work-in-progress on a scrapbook page. Begin with two textured brown cardstock backgrounds. Swipe lightly with white acrylic paint; adhere sections of torn and inked patterned papers to pages. Attach square silver brads on bottom corner of right page; stamp on date. For left page, journal on white patterned paper; cut out, treat edges with brown and black inks and adhere with silver rivet. Mat photo on inked white patterned paper mat; adhere next to journaling. Apply title with letter stickers. For right page, mat enlarged photo on white cardstock, inking edges with brown and black inks; mount on page. Adorn bottom corner with silver rivet.

Christy Tomlinson, Nampa, Idaho

Supplies: Patterned papers, tool stickers (Karen Foster Design); textured brown cardstock (Bazzill); coastal netting (Magic Mesh); letter stickers (Creative Imaginations); number stickers (Hot Off The Press); transparencies; black chalk; black brads; black floss

How To Create A Doorway

Document a construction project step by step

Scrapbook the sequences of a do-it-yourself venture to remember all the details and hard work involved. Begin with two patterned paper background pages. Apply title with letter stickers on upper corner of left page. Create a variety of peekaboo frames from brown cardstock; chalk all edges in black and tear and roll centers to expose photos beneath. Use black floss to tie back rolls and to embellish. Mat remaining photos on red, blue and brown cardstock mats. Adhere photos in sequence onto both pages. Embellish top photo on left page with coastal netting, sticker phrase and screw and nail stickers. Hang printed torn tag from photo corner. Apply number stickers on each photo to show sequence. Wrap floss around torn and chalked paper strip; adhere horizontally on right page along tops of photos. Accent one photo with nailhead stickers atop mesh strip; mount over corner. Accent both pages with various tool stickers. Journal in coordinating sequence onto transparencies; cut out and mount on both pages with black brads.

Ralonda Heston, Murfreesboro, Tennessee

Our Dirt

Fill the page with photos

Let striking photos fill up the page for a bold and graphic look. Print journaling directly onto upper corner of black cardstock background page. Use photo-editing software to print directly onto bottom corner of enlarged photo; print, cut out and adhere on page. Paint metal letters in white; sand when dry and adhere to bottom corner. Affix remaining photos on page. Adhere stitched ribbon where photos meet; mount old-fashioned key atop ribbon. Stamp phrase onto sheets of mica; heat emboss and affix on page. Ink clay word with black ink and attach to silver eyelet letters with adhesive.

Joanna Bolick, Fletcher, North Carolina

Supplies: Silver letters, silver eyelet letters (Making Memories); white craft paint (Plaid); letter stamps (PSX Design); mica tiles (USArtQuest); clay word (EK Success); key (Li'l Davis Designs); black ink; stitched ribbon; black embossing powder

Supplies: Patterned papers (Creative Imaginations); metal plaque and letters (Making Memories); letter stamps (Prickley Pear); garden cut-outs (Cardeaux)

Garden Produce

Boast a backyard harvest

Share your passion for gardening with a layout showcasing the fruits of your labor. Mat patterned paper on a green cardstock background. Tear strip of mauve patterned paper; adhere vertically along right side of page. Adorn with cut-out butterfly, flower and lizard. Mat focal photo and one secondary photo on patterned paper; adhere all on page. Create fold-out journaling tag from cream cardstock. Colorize tag using cut-out shapes and stencil; chalk images to create pattern. Adhere purple ribbon across tags; embellish with butterfly plaque and letter pebbles. Journal on vellum; cut out and mount on tags. Apply title across top of page with a variety of letters using stamps, metal letters and page pebbles.

Nicole LaCour, Memory Makers magazine

Supplies: Patterned papers (Karen Foster Design, Rusty Pickle); textured cardstock (Bazzill); mini yellow eyelets, letter pebbles, metal letter, date stamp (Making Memories); wire; walnut ink; safety pin

Harvest Point Lane

Document your home search

Record the adventure of finding a new home with pictures of you as proud new owners along with blueprint patterned papers. Begin with a patterned paper background page; adhere strip of light blue textured cardstock across top of page for title bar. Layer cut and torn sections from patterned papers vertically on page to form a pocket; set mini yellow eyelets around edges and thread wire through left side and bottom of page, curling at ends. Slip memorabilia inside. Mat two photos on textured light blue cardstock; tear one edge of each mat and adhere on page. Mount remaining photo on bottom of page. Apply title on cardstock bar with letter pebbles. Alter tag with walnut ink; apply key sticker, metal number and jump ring through hole. Attach to page with safety pin. Stamp date on tag to complete.

Shan Blake, Aliso Viejo, California

Our General Contractor

Showcase dad's handyman skills

It helps to have a dad who is an enthusiastic handyman and do-it-yourselfer. Thank him for his effort in a layout that pays tribute to his labor. Begin with a patterned paper background. Print part of title and journaling on tan cardstock; tear out and mount on page. Mat photos on tan cardstock and adhere on page. Cover two slide mounts in tan cardstock; wrap with silver wire. Hang charms from silver screw eyelets attached on slide mounts; mount on top of page. Apply brad rub-on transfers onto silver brads to complete title; attach to page and detail with black pen.

Tracy Weinzapfel Burgos, Ramona, California

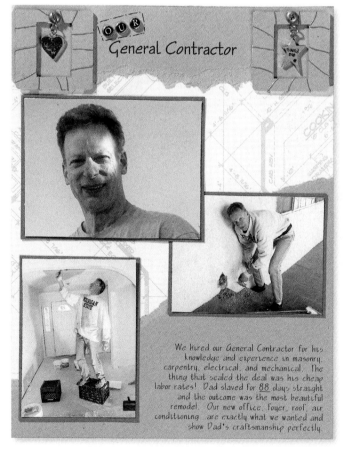

Supplies: Patterned paper (Glad Tidings); charms (Card Connection); screw eyelets (Making Memories); brad rub-on transfers (Creative Imaginations); tan cardstock; slide mounts; silver brads; silver wire

Supplies: Patterned paper (Chatterbox, 7 Gypsies); black and white cardstocks; yellow paper

…A Place Called Biff's

Show off a favorite "toy"

Record fun and fast times spent with a favorite rumbling set of wheels. Begin with two black cardstock background pages. Layer torn sections of yellow and patterned papers on left page. Triple mat photo on yellow patterned paper and white and black cardstocks, allowing for space for title. Handwrite title; mount on page. For right page, adhere cut section of patterned paper; mount on page vertically. Mat photo on black cardstock; adhere on yellow square embellished with torn section of patterned paper. Affix with unmatted photo on page. Journal on white cardstock and mount with section of yellow paper on page. Affix square-cropped photos on both pages.

Cheryl Bahneman, Acworth, Georgia

Harley Davidson

Fill the page with photos

Design a layout that packs a great deal of visual punch by filling the page almost entirely with cropped photos. Begin by enlarging one photo; adhere on black cardstock background page. Crop and mount remaining photos side by side. Journal onto metallic paper; cut out and mount on page to complete.

Veronica Hugger, Houston, Texas

Supplies: Metallic paper (Hygloss); black cardstock

Supplies: Patterned papers (7 Gypsies, Making Memories); metal photo corners, metal eyelet letter (Making Memories); vellum envelope (DMD); bubble word, oval frame, guitar and music laser-cuts (Li'l Davis Designs); white maruyama mesh (Magenta); orange mesh (Magic Mesh); black and white cardstocks; yellow and orange chalks; vellum; black brads

Neil Young & Crazy Horse

Include event memorabilia

Incorporate memorabilia from an event you attended for a keepsake page addition. Begin by adhering white patterned paper on a black cardstock background. Tear section of black patterned paper; chalk torn edges in yellow and orange and mount on page. Double mat photo on white cardstock and torn black patterned paper frame with chalked edges; accent with metal photo corners. Adhere vellum envelope on page; insert memorabilia. Embellish with bubble word mounted on oval frame. Affix laser-cut guitar on page. Mount CD facedown on page; print title on vellum, cut into strips and layer over CD with black brads. Set eyelet letter in center of CD. Layer sections of white and orange mesh vertically down page; adhere laser-cut music images over mesh.

Debbie Coe, Marysville, Ohio

Mid-life Crisis

Poke a little fun at a "phase"

They all go through the notorious midlife crisis, so make sure you put the proof in your scrapbook! Begin by cropping and matting photos on orange cardstock; adhere on a textured dark blue handmade paper background. Print enlarged title in blue ink on white cardstock; cut out, leaving white border. Adhere on page. Journal onto white cardstock; color background in orange. Cut out, leaving white border and mount on bottom of page.

MaryJo Regier, Memory Makers Books

Supplies: Textured blue handmade paper (source unknown); orange, white and blue cardstocks

3 Ponies

Show off your wheels with style

Pay tribute to your mode of transport with whimsical stickers and fun accents. Begin by rounding the corners of patterned paper; adhere on a slate-colored cardstock background. Trim dark patterned paper section and round corners; adhere on page. Braid jute cord to create border for patterned paper piece and one photo. Use letter, star and license plate stickers to create title and to embellish page. Mat all but one photo on tan and slate cardstocks; mount on page below focal photo. Trim edge of focal photo with braided jute. Detail die-cut fence with brown pen to create look of wood grain; wrap with wheat embroidery floss and adhere with foam tape.

Pamela James, Ventura, California

Supplies: Patterned papers (Hot Off The Press, My Mind's Eye); license plate stickers (Sticker Studio); fence die cut (Ellison); slate and tan cardstocks; jute; wheat embroidery floss

Truckin

Incorporate bold color blocks

A graphic look makes for a well-balanced layout and is perfect for featuring select photo elements. Begin with two textured dark purple cardstock backgrounds. Cut title vertically from light purple cardstock using die cut machine. Mat on darker cardstock strip and adhere along left side of left page. Print journaling onto vellum; cut out and adhere over light purple cardstock; accent with metal word. Adhere matted and un-matted cropped photos on page. On right page, print quote onto vellum; adhere over light purple cardstock and affix with matted and un-matted photos on page. Attach metal letters and snaps. Finish page with cut sections of cardstocks; adhere.

Vicki Garrett, Kingston, Ontario, Canada

Supplies: *Textured purple cardstocks (Bazzill); letter die cuts (Sizzix); metal letters (Making Memories); watermark ink (Tsukineko); rivets (Chatterbox); black embossing powder*

Supplies: Silver leafing pen (Krylon); metal word (Making Memories); musical charms (Paramount Music Store); heart charm (source unknown); blue and white cardstocks; tag; silver thread

Sweet Sounds

Custom create photo borders

Design photo borders from your own photos for striking page additions. Begin with two light blue cardstock backgrounds. Enlarge photos for borders; print in black-and-white and adhere along edges of both pages. Place pages side by side. Layer sections of light blue and darker blue cardstock shapes and strips that have been outlined in silver leafing pen on both pages; affix so that some shapes and lines carry over from left page to right. Print black-and-white photos with white borders; mat on light blue cardstock mats outlined with silver leafing pen and adhere to pages. Affix remaining color photos on page, matting as desired. For left page, create card from cardstock to house journaling and an additional photo. Journal on underside of cover and mount photo on interior. Attach to page; embellish cover in shapes and letters cut out from computer font and outlined in silver leafing pen. Attach silver musical note on bottom of page. Complete right page by accenting one photo with silver-lined tag hung from word eyelet and adorned with heart charm.

Sharon Whitehead, Vernon, British Columbia, Canada

Supplies: Fabric wire (Darice); musical note charm (source unknown); black and burgundy cardstocks

Wind Symphony

Feature fabroc wire letters

Fabric wire letters and musical accents make for an eye-catching, well-composed page. Begin with two burgundy cardstock background pages. For left page, affix several thin strips of black cardstock vertically along left side of page and two on right side. Use photo editing software to apply text on enlarged black-and-white photo; mat on black cardstock and adhere to page. Shape fabric wire into letters and musical notes; glue to page. Mat remaining photos on black cardstock; mount on page using foam adhesive where desired. Add musical note charm. For right page, adhere several thin strips of black cardstock on page for date, and one vertically for border on right. Apply text on top photo; mat along with remaining photos on black cardstock and mount all on page. Use fabric wire for date and remainder of title.

Sharon Whitehead, Vernon, British Columbia, Canada

Poker Night

Capture a night of fun

Supplies: Patterned papers (Amscan, Mustard Moon, Okie Dokie Press); letter stickers (EK Success); aged tags (2DYE4); white cardstock; vellum

Creatively chronicle a playful game of cards, including everyone's "poker face." Begin with orange and black patterned background pages. Layer torn and rolled sections of black cardstock, tan patterned paper and vellum vertically along left side of left page and right side of right page. Adhere cropped photos on border strips. Print captions for photos; cut into strips and adhere beneath respective photos. Mat remaining photos as desired on white cardstock; crop enlarged black-and-white photo and smaller photo so that they overlap both pages. Adhere photos. Print tile onto vellum; tear out and mount over photo on left page. Adhere letter stickers along left page border. Journal onto background page to complete.

Susan Cyrus, Broken Arrow, Oklahoma

Bingo Night

Record a favorite family ritual

Feature one of the ways your family likes to have fun with a playful and whimsical design. Begin by treating edges of a brown patterned paper background with brown ink. Create title by stamping letters onto game pieces, bottle cap, wooden letter tile, fun foam and other ephemera; mat on torn textured brown cardstock strips. Embellish with staples and rub-ons; mount on top of page. Mat photos on brown cardstock, double matting one on red cardstock and patterned paper; layer on page with portions of bingo boards. Enhance mats with metallic rub-ons. Stamp names on twill tape with brown ink; attach on corresponding photos with staples. Embellish photos with labels and fortune paper piece attached with paper clip. Sand bingo card; enhance with brown chalk and white acrylic paint in center. Journal on vellum; cut out and adhere over paint. Add staples in top corners and mount on page. Create border from label maker; affix on bottom of page along with game piece.

Jeniece Higgins, Lake Forest, Illinois

Supplies: Patterned paper (Provo Craft, Rusty Pickle); game pieces, game cards, game tickets (www.alteredpages.com); letter stamps and stencils (Hero Arts, MaVinci's, PSX Design); metallic rub-ons (Craf-T); textured brown cardstock (Bazzill); wooden letter tiles, bottle cap (Manto Fev); label maker (Dymo); white acrylic paint (Delta); vellum; fun foam; twill tape; staples; brown ink; brown chalk

Why I Do What I Do

Supplies: Wheat, brown and red cardstocks

Dedicate a page to your passion

Muse on what a special hobby such as scrapbooking means to you and how it has impacted your life. Begin with wheat-colored patterned cardstock backgrounds. For left page, enlarge photo and print two copies. Cut horizontal and vertical strips to create woven border from spare photo with craft knife and smooth cutting surface. Adhere enlarged photo to brown cardstock mat leaving, room for woven photo border; affix on page. Weave border with cut strips; mount on page along edges of photo. For right page, journal onto cardstock background, leaving room for matted photo. Mat cropped photo on red cardstock; adhere on upper corner. Align right and left pages; adhere brown cardstock section for bottom photos onto both pages. Print title onto red cardstock; cut out with craft knife and mount across both pages. Cut horizontal slits into center photo; cut vertical strips off other photos. Line up photos and weave together, gluing to adhere. Mount on bottom of pages.

Pam Kopka, New Galilee, Pennsylvania

The Best Way To Gamble...

Ante up on a poker page

Show your hand at creating a casino-style layout complete with cards, poker chips and faux cash. Begin by vertically adhering sections of red cardstock on a black cardstock background. Mat photos on white cardstock; treat edges with red ink and mount on page. Journal on white cardstock; ink edges in red and affix on page. Create title from labels and letter stamps stamped with red ink and applied on white cardstock. Ink edges of cardstock sections in red and adhere on page. Scan playing cards; print and mount on page. Embellish page with matted fake money, mini card stickers and playing chips adorned with labels.

Pam Canavan, Clermont, Florida

Supplies: Labels (Dymo); letter stamps (PSX Design); mini card stickers (EK Success); red, white and black cardstocks; red ink; faux money; poker chips

Chapter Six

RESUME – SENIOR MECHANICAL/PIPING DESIGNER

Glenn, finally after many hard years of night school, you have achieved your dream of having your Advanced Certificate in Engineering. While you have been working in this field for many years, it was a proud moment for me to see you have that valuable piece of paper in your hand. You deep insight into what you wanted to do with your life and your strength of personality to go after it, drew me to you when we first met. You have a strong and dependable air about you that let me know that this was a man I could trust to be the wonderful husband and father you have become. I will always be proud of you. Love Colleen

believe

More Than A Job □

Having a place we can look forward to going to each day that utilizes our talents is hardly a mere "job." The value of our vocations may be measured by the various ways in which both our lives and our workplaces are enriched by our efforts. From paying our dues to landing our dream jobs, we explore our capabilities and realize our own potential while on the job. Whether we are stay-at-home parents, jet-setting CEOs, just-starting-out entrepreneurs or on-our-way-up professionals, what we do for a living helps to define our unique character and personal strengths. While some choose the private sector, other career paths lead to service in the Armed Forces, where courageous individuals work to protect freedom and pursue peace. Career decisions are parts of our lives not to be missed in the pages of our scrapbook albums. In recognizing the role of our work, we acknowledge the rewards and challenges offered by every memorable occupation to which we've dedicated ourselves over the years.

At The Office?

Showcase your significant's occupation

Spotlight what makes your spouse's job special on a page that's all about what he or she does. Begin by layering two patterned papers over a stripped patterned paper background; fold over top right corner of patterned paper to expose striped background. Affix green and blue border strips along edges of patterned papers; attach molding strip over border strip with green rivet. Layer striped patterned paper and blue patterned paper sections vertically on left side of page with green rivet; mat photos on green and blue patterned papers and adhere on border. Journal on green paper; mat on blue patterned paper and affix on border. Double and single mat photos on green and blue patterned papers; mount on page. Attach folded corner over photo with green rivet. Mat business card; affix on photo. Finger-paint slide mounts using white, green and blue paints. Adhere over sections of patterned paper and mount on page. Apply letter stickers to enhanced slide mounts and tags; adhere to page with green rivets. Cut question mark from green paper; mat on blue paper and adhere to page.

Kathy Fesmire, Athens, Tennessee

Supplies: Patterned papers, border section, molding, green rivets, letter stickers, tags (Chatterbox); circle slide mount (Keller's Creations); square slide mounts (The Designer's Library); paint (Plaid); blue and green papers

Think You Want To Work In A Scrapbook Store?

Document your duties

Create journaling cards to list all the duties of your job and accompany them with photos. Begin by matting striped patterned paper on a red cardstock background. Print part of title onto a transparency; turn over and apply manila acrylic paint and adhere on top of page. Use label maker to print remainder of title; adhere at top and bottom of transparency. Using envelope template, create four envelopes from manila cardstock, inking edges slightly in red; adhere to page. Embellish envelopes with matted photos, burlap, brad and letter stickers. Journal duties on manila cardstock; mat on teal cardstock and slip into pockets to finish.

Lisa Dixon, East Brunswick, New Jersey

Supplies: Striped patterned paper (7 Gypsies); manila acrylic paint (Delta); envelope template (Deluxe Designs); letter stamps (All My Memories, K & Company); red, manila and teal cardstocks; transparency; red chalk; burlap; brad

Dream Job

Create a recessed mini album

Scrap a mini album to attach to a foam core layout to show how your dream job evolved. Cover foam core board with black paper; layer with trimmed patterned paper background. Embellish flower centers with punched circles from black and brown cardstocks. Cut section from foam core with craft knife to house mini album. Apply double-sided tape to cut-out section; adhere green ribbon and mini accordion album. Decorate album as desired using collage of items that symbolize your journey. For cover, adhere torn green paper and embellish with metal accents, stickers, ribbons, rub-on word, bookplate and silver handle. Tie ribbon around book to close. Print story onto transparency; cut out and adhere to page with photo turns and black brads. For title, use gray metallic rub-ons to enhance stencil letters; mount on page, attaching some together and accenting with green elastic and a safety pin. Hang letter tags from white elastic and jump rings from title to complete.

Diana Graham, Barrington, Illinois

Supplies: Patterned paper (Chatterbox); foam core board (Magic Scraps); mini album, photo turns, elastic (7 Gypsies); silver handle (Li'l Davis Designs); rub-on word, jump rings, label holder (Making Memories); metallic rub-ons (Craf-T); black and brown cardstocks; double-sided tape; black brads; transparency; stencil letters

Why I Love My Job

Design a design-inspired layout

Incorporating handmade fabric swatch books and paint chip borders is a great way to feature a flare for home décor and design. Begin with a tan patterned paper background. Cut paint chip sample in half; mat on red patterned paper and mount on left side and bottom of page. Affix wine cardstock strip across page; stamp additional section with script stamp and gold ink. Print title on mustard cardstock and mat on stamped background with gold eyelets; adhere on page. Punch and layer hearts from paint samples and wine cardstock on title; write title on top heart. Triple mat photo on gold and purple cardstocks and red patterned paper; machine stitch around edge of top mat and mount on page. Adhere business card along bottom of photo. Journal on mustard cardstock; cut out, mat on red patterned paper and mount on page. For mini fabric books, cut various fabrics into 2" squares with pinking shears; staple together at top, creating three different stacks. Cut wine cardstock sections for book covers slightly wider than squares and 2½" long. Score "spine" of books and set two gold eyelets; fold spine and thread gold cord through eyelets. Adhere fabric stacks inside books and mount on page. Print mini titles for books on scrap cardstock; cut out, mat on mustard cardstock and adhere on book tops.

Supplies: Patterned papers (Chatterbox); script stamp (Stampin Up!); heart punch (Family Treasures); wine and gold cardstocks; gold ink; gold eyelets; gold cord

Samantha Walker, Battle Ground, Washington

Workday

Document a day's schedule

Artfully answer the perennial question "What did you do at work today?" with a layout that lays out a typical full-time itinerary. Mat textured navy blue cardstock on a textured light blue cardstock background. Tear section of patterned paper for border; adhere vertically along left side of page. Affix strip of patterned paper atop border. Lightly chalk edges of business cards in brown; attach paper clips and adhere on border with blue brads and staples. Print events of workday on white cardstock; ink edges in brown, mat on textured light blue cardstock with staples and adhere on page. Affix sections of green cardstock and patterned paper on bottom; attach paper clip. Stamp date on tag; adhere on green strip. Cut part of title from green cardstock using computer font as a guide; complete title with computer key letters to finish.

Jennifer Bourgeault, Macomb Township, Michigan

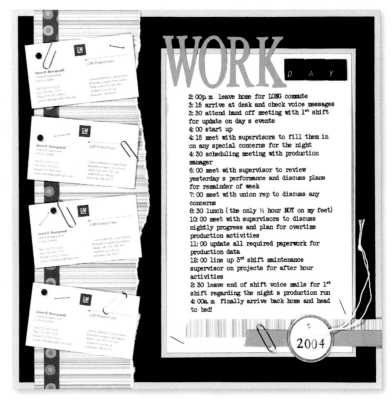

Supplies: Textured blue cardstocks (Bazzill); patterned papers (Chatterbox); computer keys (Creative Imaginations); number stamps (PSX Design); green cardstock; brown chalk; blue brads; staples; paper clips; tag

Supplies: Label holders (Anima Designs); metal letters (Making Memories); lettering templates (Scrap Pagerz); foam core board; green, purple and mustard cardstocks; craft scissors; transparency; silver brads

My Other Dream Job

Create foam core board frames

Showcase your hobby-turned-dream-job by incorporating some of the tools of your trade within foam core board frames. Begin by cutting foam core openings to display desired items; cover with purple, mustard and green cardstocks. Flip over and cut openings from cardstock using craft knife. Adhere foam core on sage cardstock background page, adhering elements to be displayed underneath such as business cards, fibers, cut-out pictures and scissors. Embellish page with green buttons tied with purple thread. Print captions and journaling onto transparency; cut out and attach to page with silver brads, placing captions under silver label holders. Use lettering templates to cut letters from yellow and gray cardstocks for part of title. Complete title with metal letters.

Torrey Miller, Thornton, Colorado

Brett Gallacher

Supplies: Patterned papers (Chatterbox, 7 Gypsies); raised numbers and word stickers, label holder, oval frame (Li'l Davis Designs); brown vellum envelope (EK Success); circles (SEI); label maker (Dymo); brown, green, red, black and tan cardstocks; paper clips

Showcase your job skills

Create a quintessential career spread complete with labels, a file folder and a copy of your current cover letter. Begin with two brown cardstock background pages. For left page, cut sections of green, tan and red cardstocks. Print on green section; embellish with patterned paper, label, cropped photo matted on black cardstock, silver label holder attached with silver brads, and raised number and word stickers. Embellish tan section with red cardstock, journaling printed on green patterned paper, brown vellum envelope, buttons, labels and raised word mounted on oval frame. Embellish red section with green circle, file folder cut from tan cardstock, script patterned paper, cropped photo matted on black cardstock attached with paper clip and labels. Adhere all sections to background page. On right page, mount yellow, tan and green circles under red folder affixed on page to form pocket for resumes. Adhere label on folder. Mount cover letter on top of folder; embellish with sections of patterned paper and buttons. Mat photo on black cardstock; accent with paper clip.

Jennifer Gallacher, Savannah, Georgia

Glass Art

Artfully display a talent

Showcase an intriguing talent with a well-composed page dedicated to celebrating the creative process. Begin with a black cardstock background. Stamp "ART" onto sienna card-stock section; heat emboss with black powder. Coat entire section with two to three layers of clear embossing enamel; when cool, bend to crack. Adhere on page. Mount cut sections of textured white and orange cardstocks along with photos on page. Attach thin black ribbon on top and bottom edge of photos. Stamp "glass" into silver metal sheet; affix on page under silver oval frame with silver brads. Journal on metal sheet with an old typewriter; affix on page to finish.

Joanna Bolick, Fletcher, North Carolina

Supplies: Textured sienna, white and orange cardstocks (Bazzill); embossing stamps (Carolee's Creations); silver metal sheets, silver oval frame (Making Memories); black cardstock; black ribbon; black and clear embossing powders; silver eyelets

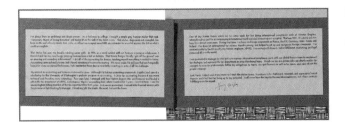

...Rising Executive

Journal your career accomplishments

Tell the story of how you got to where you are in your career with a hinged journaling booklet. Begin by journaling your story on two light purple cardstock sections; mat on purple cardstock sections. Print title on top of light purple cardstock background page; adhere section of patterned paper along bottom. Mount second portion of what will become a journaling booklet on center of background page; trim top part of journaling mat to resemble a file folder; adhere over second part of journaling with hinges. Mat focal photo on wine-colored cardstock; adhere on cover of journaling booklet along with cropped photo. Journal career highlights on white cardstock; cut out and adhere under cropped photo. Double mat business card on light purple and wine cardstocks; set eyelet at end and string fiber through, wrapping around bottom of layout and securing on back.

Nancy Korf, Portland, Oregon

Supplies: Patterned papers (Ever After); hinges (Making Memories); purple, wine and white cardstocks; eyelet; fiber

PT

Showcase his pride in his work

Have your husband describe what his job means to him in his own handwriting for a special career page keepsake. Begin by trimming vertical section of textured light blue cardstock; adhere on left side of blue cardstock background. Layer bottom of strip with textured black cardstock strip and mesh star eyelets. Crumple strips of baby blue cardstock; open, flatten and brush with white acrylic paint. Mount on page. Journal on vellum, leaving room for title tag. Thread elastic through eyelets. Tear out and adhere on top of page with silver eyelets on right side; tuck top under painted strip. Mat photos on black and blue textured cardstocks and mount on page. Stamp caption along right side of page and name onto painted strip with letter stamps. Stamp title on blue tag with letter stamps; mat on textured black cardstock and add star brad.

Valerie Barton, Flowood, Mississippi

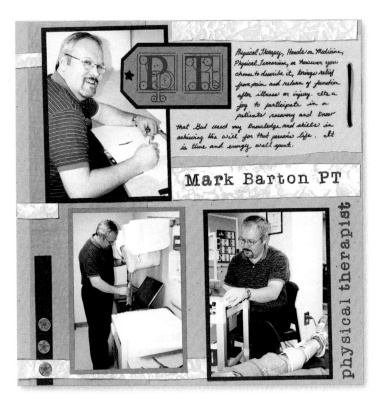

Supplies: Textured cardstock (National Cardstock); mesh star eyelets (Making Memories); letter stamps (Ma Vinci's, Stampendous); black elastic (7 Gypsies); blue cardstocks; black ink; vellum; silver eyelets

Fireplace Man

Feature found items

Collect a treasure of items to use on a page dedicated to your husband's profession. Begin by adhering strips of black cardstock vertically and horizontally on a brown patterned paper background. Use template to crop photos and make mats from black cardstock; adhere on page. Scan desired documents, seals and letterhead; reduce to desired size. Print and adhere on page with mini file folder along with cut and chalked business card. Embellish folder with mini handwritten black tag tied with red raffia. Embellish yellow cellophane with red embossing powder to resemble flames; layer with fireplace die cut and black mesh on bottom left corner. Adorn with black cardstock strip, seal and black tiles. For title bar, embellish black cardstock with a collage of found elements, chalked papers, mini tools and portion of title printed on tan cardstock. Complete title with mini tags. Machine stitch around edge and adhere to page.

MaryJo Regier, Memory Makers Books

Supplies: Patterned paper (Karen Foster Design); file folder (DMD); mini tools (Hobby Lobby); black tiles (EK Success); black cardstock; documents; seals; letterhead; mini black tag; red raffia; yellow cellophane; red embossing powder; black mesh

Involve, Inspire...

Craft photo titles

Use a photo-editing software program to turn some of your photos into eye-pleasing title bars. Begin by editing photos for title by changing the opacity to 40 percent; add text and print. Change focal photo to black-and-white; print and mat on textured black cardstock. Lay all photos and title bars on textured orange cardstock background page to determine placement of printed words; print and adhere photos and title bars. Print journaling onto textured peach cardstock; cut out and mount along bottom of page. Embellish with fabric labels affixed under ivory label holders; attach with ivory brads.

Sharon Whitehead, Vernon, British Columbia, Canada

Supplies: Textured orange, black and peach cardstocks (Bazzill); fabric labels (Me & My Big Ideas); ivory label holders (Making Memories); ivory brads

Landing A Job

Record a major milestone

Scrapbook a major development in a career path on a page that recalls the story. Begin by aging tan cardstock with walnut ink; crumple, flatten and machine stitch onto sienna cardstock background page. Adhere photos on page with photo corners; alter with purple metallic rub-ons. Journal directly onto background and highlight words with sienna rub-ons for emphasis. Scan memorabilia into Adobe Photoshop 7.0; alter colors and print. Treat further with walnut ink; adhere on page and accent with clothespin embellishment.

Rosemary Waits, Mustang, Oklahoma

Supplies: Photo corners, clothespin embellishment (Hobby Lobby); rub-ons (Making Memories); sienna and tan cardstocks; walnut ink

Paramedic Of The Year

Pay tribute to heroic efforts

Capture the career highlights and accomplishments of a loved one that showcases his or her hard work and dedication. Begin with a red, white and blue patterned paper background. Print title and journaling on a transparency; cut out and attach to page with silver brads. Adhere photo to page. Print "hero" definition on white patterned paper; mat on red patterned paper and mount on transparency. Accent with star brads. Adhere fabric label on backside of metal frame; thread with red fiber. Attach metal numbers on tags with jump rings; string onto fiber, twist and secure fiber on back of page. Adhere tagged numbers on page to keep in place.

Deborah Daunis, Santee, California

Supplies: Patterned paper (Karen Foster Design); fabric label (Me & My Big Ideas); star brads, metal numbers, metal frame (Making Memories); silver brads; red fiber, small tags; jump rings

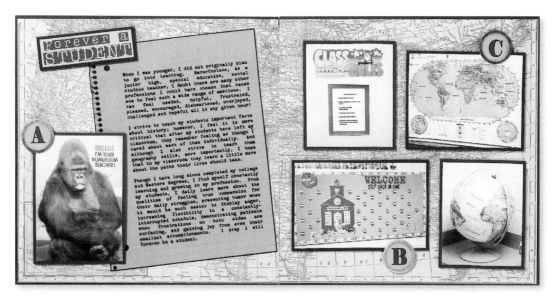

Supplies: Patterned paper (Me & My Big Ideas); faux copper tags (DMD); metallic rub-ons (Craf-T); burgundy, green, tan and red cardstocks; green paper; notebook paper; transparency; foam adhesive; black embossing powder

Forever A Student

Alter notebook paper for a school theme

Journal about the standards you hold for yourself in your job on an altered piece of notebook paper. Begin with two burgundy cardstock background pages. Frame map patterned paper on three sides with background cardstock; adhere patterned paper up to edges where pages meet. For left page, scan slightly aged notebook paper; print onto light green paper. Journal onto transparency. Trim to size of notebook paper and sprinkle with black embossing powder; heat to set. Layer onto page with notebook paper. Print title on tan cardstock; cut out, mat on red cardstock and mount on page. Tint photos in sepia tone; print, mat on green and red cardstocks, and adhere on both pages with foam adhesive. Print "A," "B" and "C" on tan cardstock; cut into circles to fit inside faux copper tags. Enhance edges with red metallic rub-ons; adhere on tags and mount on photo corners on both pages.

Denise Tucker, Versailles, Indiana

Books

Journal about what you love

If there is something about your job that you just love, journal about it. Begin with a black cardstock background; trim off right edge and adhere thin strip of gray cardstock. Print name in barcode font onto textured red cardstock; cut vertically and adhere along left side of page. Enlarge photo; trim and affix on red section. Print journaling onto black paper; cut out and mount on page. Stamp letters for title on cardstock; heat emboss with white powder. Cut out letters and layer on page with blue textured cardstock strips.

Joanna Bolick, Black Mountain, North Carolina

Supplies: Red and blue textured cardstocks (Bazzill); letter stamps (Ma Vinci's); white embossing powder; black cardstock; black paper; white ink

Army

Document a military ceremony

Preserve the pride of a special military event for a loved one in the service to remember forever. Begin by matting a piece of crumpled and torn blue patterned paper on a red cardstock background. Tear corner from camouflage paper; adhere in upper right corner. Journal on tan cardstock; tear out, chalk edges in brown and affix on bottom left corner of page. Tear section from tan cardstock; apply letter stickers for first part of title. Chalk around stickers in brown and black. Create remainder of title from dog tags strung with a beaded chain. Double mat photos on black and tan cardstocks, tearing bottom of black mats; adhere on page. Adorn one photo with gold stars cut from patterned paper.

Holle Wiktorek, Reunion, Colorado

Supplies: Patterned papers (Making Memories, Destination Paper); dog tags (Chronicle Books); red, tan and black cardstocks; chalk; beaded chain

The introduction of the black beret occurred on Flag Day, the U.S. Army's birthday. The soldiers were full of pride to show the unity and strength of our U.S. Army. I enjoyed watching the their proud faces as the canon fired, Color Guard presented, air show team performed and General Cody spoke. Each "one" of our soldiers has an important role to perform in our fight for freedom.
Ft. Campbell, Kentucky   June 14, 2001

United States Navy

Incorporate journaling booklets into a page

Create a biographical layout with detailed booklets that tell the story of your or a loved one's military service. Begin by cutting top and bottom from flag patterned paper; adhere on red patterned paper background. Form pocket for larger journaling booklet by machine stitching the top and bottom of page onto a strap-hinge-style page. Affix torn vellum to top of page with gold brads; string with gold wire. Attach gold anchor to precut title with jump ring; mount on vellum and accent with Navy seal accent. For book-style journaling, print story onto ivory paper; cut into small pages. Create cover from blue cardstock and embellish with patterned paper, matted photo and title strip mounted with gold eyelets. Add ribbon, gold star and gold Navy accent with red brads. Layer over pages and attach with gold brads and gold wire. Embellish remainder of page with additional Navy memorabilia. Print additional journaling onto ivory paper at full size; bind by machine stitching a patterned paper edge across gathered pages. Slip booklet into pocket.

Pamela James, Ventura, California

Supplies: Patterned papers, metal accents (K & Company); precut title (Scrappix); gold anchor (Avon); ivory paper; vellum; red and gold brads; ribbon; gold eyelets

Supplies: Patterned red, white and blue cardstocks (Club Scrap); silver star eyelets; vellum

If You Think Of Me

Dedicate a layout to a loved one in the service

Feature tender sentiments to reflect feelings toward a far away loved one serving in the military. Begin with red, white and blue patterned cardstocks. For left page, tear blue cardstock; adhere on red background. Print title and journaling onto vellum; cut, tear out and adhere on page. Mat top photo on white cardstock; affix along with un-matted photo on page. Embellish page with star eyelets. For right page, layer torn white and red cardstock sections on blue cardstock background. Adhere photos on page; affix torn blue cardstock strip next to top photo. Mat cropped photo on red cardstock; mount with foam adhesive on top photo. Print excerpt from lyrics onto vellum; cut out and mount on page. Accent page with star eyelets to complete.

Ari Macias, Staten Island, New York
Photos: Guillermo Macias, Staten Island, New York

Think of me everyday, hold tight to what I say and I'll be close to you, even from faraway. Know that wherever you are, it is never too far. If you think of me, I'll be with you....

Phil Vischer
From the Veggietales movie Rack, Shack and Benny

Supplies: Patterned paper (Colorbök); Sonja alphabet (QuicKutz); number sticker (Wordsworth); letter stamps (PSX Design); crown stamp (Anna Griffin); clock stamp (Postmodern Design); red and blue cardstocks; white and black inks; gold brads

Only 2 Weeks

Record time spent during R & R leave

How you spent two precious weeks together after being separated for so long is something you will both want to remember forever. Begin with two patterned paper backgrounds. For left page, mat photos on red cardstock; adhere top photos on blue cardstock, stamp caption with white ink and letter stamps and mount all on background page. Print journaling onto light blue cardstock; mat on red cardstock and adhere on page. Apply title with punched letters; adhere on blue cardstock strip with "2" sticker affixed on cardstock circle treated with blue chalk. Mount on page. Use letter stamps to create captions inside patterns of background paper; add various-sized gold brads. For right page, use craft knife to cut slits in circles of patterned paper background to insert matted photo corners. Mat photos on red cardstock and mount on page. Stamp words directly on page; add gold brads. Stamp clock and crown images on red cardstock circles; adhere on page.

Holle Wiktorek, Reunion, Colorado

A Bird's-Eye View...

Paint a watercolor background

Try your hand at re-creating a photo background with watercolors. Begin by painting background on watercolor paper; tear out and adhere to a red cardstock background. Mat photos on tan cardstock; affix on page. Adhere military patch to center of page. Cut rectangle section from blue cardstock; adhere torn section from painted watercolor paper and mount on upper left corner of page. Stamp title in black ink with letter stamps. Journal along right side of page and bottom portion of photo with gold pen.

Samantha Walker, Battle Ground, Washington

Supplies: Watercolor paper (Arches); watercolors (Windsor & Newton); letter stamps (Stampin' Up!); red, tan and blue cardstocks; military patch; black ink; gold pen

Supplies: Metal letters, mesh star eyelets (Making Memories); burgundy and blue cardstocks; clear photo protector; fabric; red floss; uniform buttons; vellum; skeleton leaves

Courage, Commitment, Honor

Sew a fabric frame

Protect an old photo and display it beautifully all at once by using a piece of fabric for a frame. Begin with a burgundy cardstock background; layer photo on page with dark blue cardstock, crumpled burgundy cardstock and a clear protector to go over photo. Cut opening in fabric for frame; roll openings back and secure by threading red floss through bottom behind rolls and over rolls, tying to secure. Adhere fabric frame over photo; machine stitch around fabric edge. Using an "X" pattern, machine stitch around entire page. Adhere uniform buttons on corners of frame. Print Sailor's Creed and name onto vellum; attach on opposite corners with mesh star eyelets. On remaining corners, attach skeleton leaves with mesh star eyelets. Adhere title with metal letters.

Andrea Lyn Vetten-Marley, Aurora, Colorado

Courage

Journal a loved one's military memories

Record a veteran's wartime recollections and emotions stirred by a particular photograph taken during his or her service. Begin by tearing section of military patterned paper; alter torn edges with brown and charcoal metallic rub-ons. Cut section from script patterned paper; treat edges with brown metallic rub-ons. Layer onto a green patterned paper background along with torn military section, brown mesh, tank laser cut and script patterned paper section. Double mat photo on brown cardstock and script patterned paper mat; treat edges with brown metallic rub-ons. Mount on page, adhering right side and bottom only to form pocket for tag. Journal on manila tag; treat with brown metallic rub-ons and accent with altered brad. Slip tag behind photo. Poke holes in faux eyelets on page; string dog tag onto beaded chain and through poked holes, securing on back of page. Embellish with Army medal, safety pins, raised word affixed in oval frame and knotted gold ribbon attached across photo with staples.

Cindy Harris, Modesto, California

Supplies: Patterned papers (Karen Foster Design, 7 Gypsies); rub-ons (Craf-T); brown mesh (Magic Mesh); tank laser cut, dog tag, chain, safety pins, Army medal, bubble word, oval frame (Li'l Davis Designs); brown cardstock; tag; gold ribbon; staples

...The U.S.S. Independence

Incorporate industrial page elements

Give an industrial look to a navy-themed layout with washers, grommets and a metal-hinged booklet. Begin by adhering corrugated paper on a cardboard background. Affix white and blue cardstock strips and a red cardstock oval together with silver grommets; adhere across top of page. Print title on white cardstock; mat on blue cardstock and adhere to strip. Vertically affix red section cut from cardstock on left side of page; mount photos matted on blue cardstocks atop it. Cut two pieces from blue cardstock for book; attach patterned paper pocket to back page with silver eyelets. Mat photo for cover on blue and red cardstocks; cut and crumple patterned paper section and adhere on mat. Set silver eyelets inside washers; mount on blue cardstock strip and adhere over crumpled patterned paper piece. Attach piano hinge to both pages with silver grommets; affix backside onto page. Line inside of front page with corrugated paper. Journal on vellum; sprinkle with black embossing powder and heat to set. Adhere over corrugated paper and accent with blue and red cardstock squares. Slip memorabilia in pocket. Journal below photo.

Samantha Walker, Battle Ground, Washington

Supplies: Corrugated paper (FLAX Art & Design); eyelets (Prym Dritz); patterned paper (Frances Meyer, Chatterbox); cardboard; piano hinge; white, blue and red cardstocks; vellum; silver eyelets

I Love My Top Gun

Form a metal letter title

Metal letters make for perfect title accents on a military-themed page. Tear sections of green faux eyelet patterned paper and star patterned paper; adhere vertically on military background paper. Poke holes in faux eyelets and string with black twine. Double and single mat photos on brown and chocolate brown cardstocks. Crop small photo to fit under metal frame; adhere all photos to page. Create title from metal letters and letter tags affixed with silver brads; add metal heart set with silver eyelet. Mat name on torn piece of brown cardstock. Embellish page with stickers to complete.

Linda Cummings, Murfreesboro, Tennessee

Supplies: Patterned papers, stickers (Karen Foster Design); metal frame (Scrapworks); metal letters and tags (Creative Imaginations, Making Memories); brown cardstocks; black twine; silver brads; silver eyelets

Military Man

Feature a single favorite photo

Complement a favorite photo of a family member serving in the military with just the right patterned paper. Begin with a military patterned paper background; mat photo on same paper. Adhere matted photo on tan cardstock; treat edges with black ink. Cut photo corners from tan cardstock; ink edges in black and affix over corners of photo. Adorn corners with star brads; mount completed piece on page. Cut section from tan cardstock for title bar; ink edges in black and apply metal letters. Mount on page. Journal on tan cardstock; cut into strips, ink edges in black and adhere to page.

Jennifer Miller, Humble, Texas

Supplies: Patterned paper (Rusty Pickle); metal letters, star brads (Making Memories); tan cardstock; black ink

Proudly Serving The USA

Print on canvas paper

Print a photo and journaling onto canvas paper to add the perfect texture to an Army-themed page. Begin by tearing corner section of sand-colored patterned cardstock; adhere on tan patterned paper background. Print journaling, "top ten" reasons and photo onto canvas paper. Cut out "top ten" list; poke holes along right side. String with twine and mat on crumpled and torn patterned paper; adhere on upper left corner of page. Set eyelets in corners of photo; string with twine, dog tags, mat on burlap and mount on bottom right corner. Chalk journaling in brown and gold; mat on copper mulberry and adhere on page. Embellish upper right corner with pieces of gold mesh, metal star tied with twine, corrugated paper scrap, square eyelet and cork piece; write "hero" on cork and wrap with twine. For title, attach canvas tag to metal star; adhere on page. Tear section from mulberry, stamp portion of title in brown ink and mount beneath star. Hang square tag from twine with gold brad. Form letters from paper yarn; adhere on page. Write remainder of title on tags and stamp date on bottom right side of page to complete.

Holle Wiktorek, Reunion, Colorado

Supplies: Patterned paper (Creative Imaginations); canvas photo paper (Fedrix); dog tags (Chronicle Books); mulberry (PrintWorks); eyelets, cork (Creative Imaginations); gold mesh (JewelCraft); paper yarn and metal stars (Making Memories); letter stamps (Hero Arts); golden patterned cardstock; twine; chalk; burlap; date stamp; gold brad

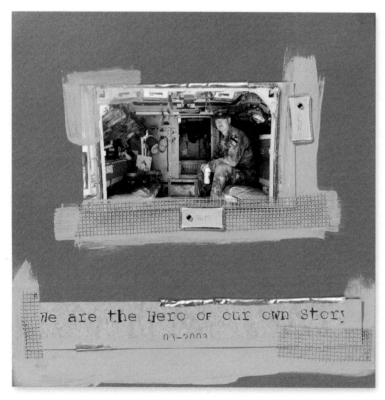

Supplies: Acrylic paint (Plaid); mini metal letter stamps (Foofala); brown and rust cardstocks; silver scrap metal; drywall screening; vellum tags; brown ink; silver brads

We Are The Hero Of Our Own Story

Paint a photo frame

Use bold strokes of acrylic paint to create a unique framing effect directly onto your page. Begin with a brown cardstock background page. Fold silver scrap metal randomly over photo edges; mount on page. Affix drywall screening across bottom of photo; using wide brush, apply moss green acrylic paint over edges of photo and onto background to create frame. Using mini metal letter stamps and brown ink, apply words on vellum tags; attach with silver brads. Print title and date on rust-colored cardstock; cut out and randomly place scrap metal over edges. Adhere on bottom of page with drywall screening; paint, covering parts of title.

Michelle Miller, Killeen, Texas

Supplies: Textured blue cardstock (Bazzill); page pebble (Making Memories); khaki and red cardstocks; large gold brads

My Hero

Honor a loved one's military commitment

Commemorate how a loved one is a hero of our nation and a hero to you personally by expressing your appreciation in heartfelt journaling. Begin by journaling onto khaki cardstock, leaving room at bottom for matted photo. Cut out and adhere on a textured blue cardstock background; accent with large gold brads at top. Cover word "hero" with page pebble. Print tile on khaki cardstock; mat on red cardstock and attach to center of page with large gold brads. Adhere un-matted photos on page. Mat cropped photo on red cardstock; adhere at bottom of journaling box.

Michelle Miller, Killeen, Texas

U.S. Army

Include an army patch accent

Add accents like army patches for the perfect military page embellishments. Begin with a green cardstock background; mat photos on extra long tan cardstock mats. Mount matted photos on page along with Army patch attached with gold brads. Apply "courage" sticker on top of bottom photo. Embellish mats with wire mesh, letter stickers, stamp stickers, faux metal tag hung on beaded chain and tag adorned with fiber and sticker. Use foam adhesive where desired for dimension. Treat definition sticker with walnut ink and mat on textured brown cardstock. Print caption on tan cardstock; age with walnut ink and mount above definition with gold brads. Journal on tan cardstock and ink in brown; mat on brown textured cardstock, embellish with stamp stickers and adhere on upper right corner of page. Hang faux metal cut-out tag with beaded chain; layer on page with sticker and section of textured brown cardstock.

Michelle Miller, Killeen, Texas

Supplies: Textured brown cardstock (Bazzill); courage sticker, postage stickers, letter stickers (EK Success); tags, stickers (K & Company); green and tan cardstocks; gold brads; army patch; wire mesh; gold chain; walnut ink

Additional credits and instructions

Cover Always And Forever

Begin with two black cardstock backgrounds. Adhere trimmed light blue cardstock to left background and red trimmed cardstock to right background. Make custom page corners from scanning pattern in shirt; adhere. Affix vertical strip of red cardstock onto left side of page. Print title segments onto pink and blue cardstock. Tear "always"; ink edges and layer over torn white textured cardstock. Cut remaining segments with craft knife; mount with flower stickers. Color white textured cardstock with pink, blue and red chalks. Line up both pages; affix various torn strips of pink and blue cardstocks and white textured cardstock, overlapping both pages. Embellish strips with fiber, charms and beads; cut down center to separate. For left page, double mat photo to red and pink cardstock; add blue cardstock and metal photo corners to top of frame. Tie black ribbon on bottom of photo. Make definition framed tags from pink and blue cardstock; hang from frame with metal swirl clip and beaded fiber. Mount photo to page with triple-thick foam tape. Create collage embellishment from various papers matted onto black cardstock. Enhance with beads, fibers, embellished tag, clock face and metal heart charm. For right page, layer large sections of textured cardstock and blue cardstocks with chalked edges. Double mat focal photo to red and black cardstock, tearing right side of black mat; adhere to page with triple-thick foam tape and smaller matted photo. Print "always" and "forever" vertically onto floral paper journaling boxes; adhere printed journaling on boxes and mat to blue cardstock. Tear left and top edges of mat; chalk torn edges red. Adhere to top of page. Finish page with flower stickers.

Kelly Angard, Highlands Ranch, Colorado

Supplies: Cardstock (Bazzill); texture flower paper (source unknown); flower stickers (EK Success); word beads (Magnetic Poetry); clock face (source unknown); decorative metal photo corners (Nunn Design); circle clip (Making Memories); metal charm (source unknown)

Page 3 Bookplate

Trim and mat sky blue cardstock on navy blue cardstock. Tear one side of textured pink cardstock strip; ink edges in black. Layer with cut strip of textured raspberry cardstock and torn section of embossed paper; treat paper with dark pink, light pink and light blue chalks. String fiber with wire clip and vellum tag; write "love" on tag and ink edges. Further accent with watch face, additional fibers and flower stickers. Secure fibers to back and mount on sky blue cardstock.

Torrey Miller, Thornton, Colorado

Supplies: Textured paper (Jennifer Collection); flower stickers (EK Success); watch face (Limited Edition Rubberstamps); vellum tag (Stampendous!); wire clip (7 Gypsies); chalk ink; fibers; chalk; navy blue, sky blue, pink and raspberry cardstocks

Page 6 My One True Love

Trim green patterned paper; mat on dark green cardstock background. Adhere pressed flowers along bottom with spray adhesive; cover with transparent patterned sticker. Wrap green and yellow ribbons vertically on left side of patterned paper, threading through ribbon charm; mount on cardstock background. Print title and journaling on clear transparency; cut out and paint on back with yellow acrylic paint. Mat photo on light green cardstock; wrap with ribbons and ribbon charm and affix on page along with title and journaling. Adorn page with pressed flowers and skeleton leaves.

Supplies: Patterned paper (K & Company); dried flowers, skeleton leaves (Nature's Pressed); spray adhesive (Helmar); transparent patterned sticker (Tumblebeasts); ribbon charms (Making Memories); acrylic paint (Delta); green cardstock; ribbons

Page 12 To Be Me

Begin with a patterned paper background page. Create a collage with tickets, a license plate sticker, various papers, playing card accents, definitions, words, sanded red label holder and corrugated cardboard. Tear out and sand words to alter. Treat additional papers and card accents with charcoal chalk and rub-ons. Stamp date onto one card. Attach cardboard to page with staples and silver photo turns attached with gold brads. Double mat photo on altered patterned paper and white cardstock; rub edges with charcoal rub-ons, rolling in various spots. Mat letters for title on black cardstock; adhere at askew angle on corrugated cardboard section. Affix rub-on word at top of page.

Carla Jacobsen, Lebanon, Tennessee
Photos: Karen S. Hill of Crossroads Photography & Design, Lebanon, Tennessee

Supplies: Patterned papers (K & Company, Li'l Davis Designs); tickets, license plate sticker, green corrugated cardboard (MPR Associates); luster rub-ons (Craf-T); words, silver photo turns (7 Gypsies); staples (Swingline); date stamp, rub-on word (Making Memories); red label holder, title letters (Li'l Davis Designs); black and white cardstocks; gold brads; chalk

Page 30 The Power Of One

Print journaling directly onto textured tan cardstock background. Print part of title onto bottom of patterned paper. Cut into vertical section and machine sew onto background page. Cut a strip of patterned paper to go under and along bottom of photo. Ink edges of patterned paper with brown ink and adhere to underside of photo; mount to lower right side of page. Tie vanilla ribbon around top and bottom of page; add silver double heart charm to top ribbon. Cut square section of patterned paper; cut four large hearts using craft knife and heart template. Ink inside of hearts and outside edges of square in brown. Use a photo-editing software program to apply title to flower photos before printing. Print, cut out and adhere to page under punched openings. Add silver charm to center. Finish by framing a small photo section in silver tag; affix to lower right side of page.

Mellette Berezoski, Crosby, Texas

Supplies: Textured tan cardstock (Bazzill); patterned paper (Magenta, 7 Gypsies); charms (Lone Star Scrapbooks); heart template (Making Memories); square tag (Making Memories); brown ink; vanilla ribbon

Page 50 Family Is Everything

Ink edges of patterned white paper with brown ink; adhere to green cardstock background page. Layer with green cheesecloth, copper coastal netting and lace trim. Mat photo on green cardstock; tear out, treat edges with brown ink and mount on page. Affix definition sticker across top of photo and attach black photo turns with brads. Journal onto cream cardstock; tear out and ink edges in brown. Wrap left side with inked fiber; tie off with charm and mount on page. Age large tag with walnut ink; wrap inked twill tape around bottom and alter edges of tag with black ink. Tie cheesecloth around right edge and attach mesh strip to top of tag. Form first part of title from inked and stamped jewelry tags; affix to large tag over mesh with brads. Apply remainder of title with stamps and letter stickers. Accent tag with rustic heart wrapped in fiber. Adhere tag to page. Affix word stickers along mesh border. Stamp date on bottom of page.

Trudy Sigurdson, Victoria British Columbia, Canada

Supplies: Patterned paper (Creative Imaginations); copper mesh (Magic Mesh); definition sticker, black page turns, date stamp (Making Memories); heart charm (Blue Moon Beads); letter stamps (PSX Design); letter stickers (Me & My Big Ideas); rust heart (Provo Craft); word stickers (K & Company); patterned white cardstock; green and cream cardstocks; brown and black ink; walnut ink; shipping tag; jewelry tags; cheesecloth; twill tape; lace trim; brads; fiber

Page 70 Friends

Tie your layout together with stitching to symbolize the ties that bind a long-distance friendship. Begin by treating edges of sections of textured green and purple cardstocks with watermark ink. Repeat inking technique on purple handmade paper and green velvet paper; layer all on page, machine stitching each section separately as you mount. Machine stitch photos on inked velvet and handmade paper; adhere on page. Affix light green mesh across top of page; trim edges with purple ribbon. Cut title with craft knife using computer font as a guide; chalk letters in purple and coat with dimensional adhesive. Affix letters over mesh; use letter stamps to stamp "friends" on aged washer. Adhere mesh on bottom left side of page; trim with purple ribbon and embellish with word tokens. Journal on light purple mulberry; cut out and mount on page. Embellish page with metal stars.

Shannon Taylor, Bristol, Tennessee

Supplies: Textured light green and purple cardstocks (Bazzill); handmade paper (Artistic Scrapper); velvet paper (Wintech); watermark ink (Stampin' Up!); mesh (Magic Scraps); dimensional adhesive (Sakura Hobby Craft); letter stamps (All Night Media); word tokens (Junkitz); metal stars (Anima Designs); purple ribbon

Page 88 Fishing Is Not A Hobby

Tear sides from tan patterned paper; treat edges with brown ink. Layer along with blue cardstock onto tan cardstock background page. Ink edges of background in brown. Adhere strip of netting across page; string fiber through top end and around top of page. Cut photo into sections in the same width as openings of netting; weave through and adhere. Mat focal photo on blue cardstock; mount on page with foam adhesive. Stamp title onto sections of linen cloth in dark brown ink; use metal letters in place of stamps as desired. Attach to page with eyelets. Create name from metal words applied on linen scrap; tie onto large metal washer, attach fishing hook swivel on knot and adhere to page. Embellish remainder of page with square clips, fish hooks, fishing swivels and fishing vest accent.

Andrea Lyn Vetten-Marley, Aurora, Colorado

Supplies: Patterned paper (Me & My Big Ideas); netting (Designer's Library); letter stamps (Stamp Craft); linen cloth (Charles Craft); metal letters, washer words, date tag, square clips (Making Memories); fishing vest accent (Hobby Lobby); blue and tan cardstocks; brown ink; fibers; eyelets; large metal washer; fish hooks; fish swivels

Page 106 Resume

Create a dimensional and complex-looking layout with layers of patterned papers and a printed transparency overlay. Begin with a lavender handmade paper background. Layer torn and cut sections of purple patterned paper, a printed resume and collage elements onto page. Treat all page elements and paper edges with black ink. Adhere left edge of transparency onto background page with black brads. Cut and tear corner section from black quilted paper; attach brads along straight edges and affix onto transparency. Adhere photo on quilted paper; mat smaller photo on black cardstock and adhere to transparency layer. Print journaling onto ivory cardstock; ink edges and mat on lavender cardstock. Adhere over photo. Print phrases on patterned paper; cut into strips, treat edges with black ink and adhere along with clock faces onto transparency. Ink printed "believe" ribbon and attach to page over strips with black brads.

Colleen Macdonald, Calgary Alberta, Canada

Supplies: Lavender handmade paper (Provo Craft); patterned papers (Karen Foster Design); transparency overlay (K & Company); black quilted paper (Fossil); believe ribbon (7 Gypsies); clock faces (DMD); black ink; black brads

Contributing Memory Makers Masters:

Valerie Barton, Joanna Bolick, Jennifer Bourgeault, Susan Cyrus, Kathy Fesmire, Diana Graham, Andrea Lyn Vetten-Marley, Torrey Miller, Trudy Sigurdson, Denise Tucker, Sharon Whitehead, Holle Wiktorek

Sources

The following companies manufacture workspace and storage products featured in this book. Please check your local retailers to find these materials, or go to a company's Web site for the latest product. In addition, we have made every attempt to properly credit the items mentioned in this book. We apologize to any company that we have listed incorrectly, and we would appreciate hearing from you.

2DYE4
(519) 537-6756
www.canscrapink.com

7 Gypsies
(480) 325-3358
www.7gypsies.com

Accu-Cut® (wholesale only)
(800) 288-1670
www.accucut.com

Adobe
www.adobe.com

All My Memories
(888) 553-1996
www.allmymemoreis.com

All Night Media- see Plaid Enterprises

American Art Clay Co. (AMACO)
(800) 374-1600
www.amaco.com

American Crafts (wholesale only)
(800) 879-5185
www.americancrafts.co

American Traditional™ Stencils
(800) 278-3624
www.americantraditional.com

Amscan, Inc.
(800) 444-8887
www.amscan.com

Anima Designs
9800) 570-6847
www.animadesigns.com

Anna & Bess- no contact info available

Anna Griffin, Inc. (wholesale only)
(888) 817-8170
www.annagriffin.com

Arches- no contact info available

Artistic Expressions
(219) 764-5158
www.artisticexpressionsinc.com

Artistic Scrapper
(818) 786-8304
www.artisticscrapper.com

Autumn Leaves (wholesale only)
(800) 588-6707
www.autumnleaves.com

Avon
www.avon.com

Bazzill Basics Paper
(480)558-8557
www.bazzillbasics.com

Bead Treasures- no contact info available

Beads & Plenty More- no contact info available

Blue Moon Beads
(800) 377-6715
www.beads.net

Bo-Bunny Press
(801) 771-0481
www.bobunny.com

Books By Hand/Solum World Paper
(505) 255-3534

Boutique Trims, Inc.
(248) 437-2017
www.boutiquetrims.com

Broderbund Software
(319) 247-3325
www.broderbund.com

Canson, Inc.®
(800) 628-9283
www.canson-us.com

Card Connection- see Michaels Arts & Crafts

Cardeaux®
(800) 226-8905

Carolee's Creations®
(435) 563-1100
www.carolees.com

Charles Craft- no contact info available

Chatterbox, Inc.
(208) 939-9133
www.chatterboxinc.com

Chronicle Books
www.chroniclebooks.com

Close To My Heart®
(888) 655-6552
www.closetomyheart.com

Cloud 9 Design
(763) 493-0990
www.cloud9design.biz

Club Scrap™, Inc.
(888) 634-9100
www.clubscrap.com

Coloramics, LLC
(614) 876-1171
www.magicmetallics.com

Colorbök™, Inc. (wholesale only)
(800) 366-4660
www.colorbok.com

Crafter's Workshop, The
(877) CRAFTER
www.thecraftersworkshop.com

Craf-T Products
(507) 235-3996
www.craf-tproducts.com

Creative Imaginations (wholesale only)
(800) 942-6487
www.cigift.com

Creative Memories®
(800) 468-9335
www.creativememories.com

Cropper Hopper
(800) 826-8806
www.cropperhopper.com

Current®, Inc.
(800) 848-2848
www.currentinc.com

Daisy D's Paper Company
(888) 601-8955
www.daisydspaper.com

Darice, Inc.
(800) 321-1494
www.darice.com

DecoArt™
www.decoart.com

Delta Technical Coatings, Inc.
(800)423-4135
www.deltacrafts.com

Deluxe Designs
(480) 497-9005
www.deluxecuts.com

DeNami Design Rubber Stamps
(253) 437-1626

Design Originals
(800) 877-7820
www.d-originals.com

Designer's Library, The
(660) 582-6484
www.thedesignerslibrary.com

DiBona Designs- no contact info available

DieCutsWith A View™
(877) 221-6107
www.diecutswithaview.com

Dizzy Frizzy- no contact info available

DMD Industries, Inc. (wholesale only)
(800) 805-9890
www.dmdind.com

Doodlebug Design Inc.™
(801) 952-0555
www.doodlebugdesigninc.com

Dymo
www.dymo.com

EK Success™, Ltd. (wholesale only)
(800) 524-1349
www.eksuccess.com

Ellison® Craft & Design
(800) 253-2238
www.ellison.com

Ever After Scrapbook Co.
(800) 646-0010

Family Treasures®, Inc.
www.familytreasures.com

Fiskars, Inc. (wholesale only)
(715) 842-2091
www.fiskars.com

FLAX Art & Design
(800) 343-FLAX
www.flaxart.com

Foofala
(402) 330-3208
www.foofala.com

Fossil- no contact info available

Frances Meyer, Inc.
(800) 372-6237
www.francesmeyer.com

Fredrix Artist Canvas (wholesale only)
www.fredrixartistcanvas.com

Glad Tidings, Inc.
(800) 524-5214
www.gladtidingspapers.com

Global Solutions
(206) 343-5210
www.globalsolutionsonline.com

Grafix® Graphic Art Systems, Inc.
(wholesale only)
(800) 447-2349
www.grafixarts.com

Graphic Products Corporation
(800) 323-1660
www.gpcpapers.com

Hampton Art Stamps, Inc.
(800) 229-1019
www.hamptonart.com

Helmar Australia
www.helmar.com.au

Hero Arts® Rubber Stamps, Inc.
(wholesale only)
(800) 882-4376
www.heroarts.com

Hirschberg Schutz & Co. (wholesale only)
(800) 221-8640

Hobby Lobby
www.hobbylobby.com

Hot Off The Press, Inc.
(800) 227-9595
www.paperpizzazz.com

Hygloss Products, Inc.
(201) 458-1700

Impress Rubber Stamps
(206) 901-9101
www.impressrubberstamps.com

Inkadinkado® Rubber Stamps
(800) 888-4652
www.inkadinkado.com

It Takes Two®
(800) 331-9843
www.ittakestwo.com

Jennifer Collection, The
(518) 272-4572

Jesse James & Co., Inc.
(610) 435-0201
www.jessejamesbutton.com

Jest Charming
www.jestcharming.com

JewelCraft, LLC
(201) 223-0804
www.jewelcraft.biz

JudiKins
(310) 515-1115
www.judikins.com

Junkitz
(212) 944-4250
www.junkitz.com
K & Company
(888) 244-2083
www.kandcompany.com
Karen Foster Design™ (wholesale only)
(801) 451-9779
www.karenfosterdesign.com
Keller's Creations- no contact info available
KI Memories
www.kimemories.com
Krylon
(216) 566-2000
www.krylon.com
Lasting Impressions for Paper, Inc.
(801) 298-1979
www.lastingimpressions.com
Li'l Davis Designs
(949) 838-0344
www.lildavisdesigns.com
Lifetime Moments- no contact info available
Limited Edition Rubberstamps
(650) 594-4242
www.limitededitionrs.com
Liquitex® Artist materials
(888) 4ACRYLIC
www.liquitex.com
Lone Star Scrapbooks- no contact info available
Lowe's
www.lowes.com
Magenta Rubber Stamps (wholesale only)
(800) 565-5254
www.magentarubberstamps.com
Magic Mesh™
(651) 345-6374
www.magicmesh.com
Magic Scraps™
(972) 238-1838
www.magicscraps.com
Magnetic Poetry, Inc.
www.magneticpoetry.com
Making Memories
(800) 286-5263
www.makingmemories.com
Manto Fev
(402) 321-2264
www.mantofev.com
Marshall Company, The
(800) 621-5488
www.bkaphoto.com
Maude and Millie- no contact info available
Ma Vinci's Reliquary
www.crafts.dm
Me & My Big Ideas (wholesale only)
(949) 589-4607
www.meandmybigideas.com
Memories Complete™, LLC
(866) 966-6365
www.memoriescomplete.com
Michaels® Arts & Crafts
(800) 642-4235
www.michaels.com
Microsoft
www.microsoft.com
Modern Options- no contact info available
MPR Associates, Inc.
(336) 861-6343
Mrs. Grossman's Paper Co. (wholesale only)
(800) 429-4549
www.mrsgrossmans.com
Mustard Moon™
(408) 229-8542
www.mustardmoon.com
My Mind's Eye™, Inc.
(801) 298-3709
www.frame-ups.com
National Cardstock
(724) 452-7120
www.nationalcardstock.com

Nature's Pressed
(800) 850-2499
www.naturespressed.com
Nunn Design
(360) 379-3557
www.nunndesign.com
Office Max
www.officemax.com
Okie-Dokie Press, The
(801) 298-1028
Paper Adventures® (wholesale only)
(800) 727-0699
www.paperadventures.com
Paper Company™, The
(800) 426-8989
www.thepaperco.com
Paper Fever, Inc.
(801) 328-3560
www.paperfever.com
Pakon®, Inc.
(866) 227-1229
www.pakon.com
Pebbles, Inc.®
(800) 438-8153
www.pebblesinc.com
Pewter Accents- no contact info available
Pioneer Photo Albums, Inc.®
(800) 366-3686
www.pioneerphotoalbums.com
Plaid Enterprises, Inc.
(800) 842-4197
www.plaidonline.com
Postmodern Design
(405) 321-3176
Pressed Petals, Inc.
(800) 748-4656
Prickley Pear Rubber Stamps
www.prickleypear.com
PrintWorks
(800) 854-6558
www.printworkscollection.com
Provo Craft® (wholesale only)
(888) 577-3545
www.provocraft.com
Prym-Dritz Corporation
www.dritz.com
PSX Design™
(800) 782-6748
www.psxdesign.com
Pulsar Paper Products
(877) 861-0031
www.pulsarpaper.com
QuicKutz®
(888) 702-1146
www.quickutz.com
Ranger Industries, Inc.
9800) 244-2211
www.rangerink.com
Rubber Stampede
(800) 423-4135
www.rubberstampede.com
Rusty Pickle
www.rustypickle.com
Sakura Hobby Craft
(310) 212-7878
www.sakuracraft.com
Scrap Ease®
(800) 272-3874
www.whatsnewltd.com
Scrap Pagerz™
(435) 645-0696
wwww.scrappagerz.com
Scrappin' Safari- no contact info available
Scrappix
(866) 444-8997
www.scrappix.com
Scrapworks, LLC
(801) 363-1010
www.scrapworksllc.com

Scrapyard 329
(775) 829-1118
www.scrapyard329.com
SEI, Inc.
(800) 333-3279
www.shopsei.com
Sizzix
(866) 742-4447
www.sizzix.com
Stampabilities
(800) 888-0321
www.stampabilities.com
Stampcraft- see Plaid Enterprises
Stampendous!®
(800) 869-0474
www.stampendous.com
Stampin' Up!®
(800) 782-6787
www.stampinup.com
Stampington & Company
(877) STAMPER
Stamps by Judith
www.stampsbyjudith.com
Stanley Classic Brassware- no contact
info available
Staples
www.staples.com
Sticker Studio
(208) 322-2465
www.stickerstudio.com
Style-a-bility- no contact info available
Sunday International
www.sundayint.com
Suze Weinberg Design Studio
(732) 761-2400
www.schmoozewithsuze.com
Swingline
www.swingline.com
Target
www.target.com
Treasured Memories- no contact info available
Treehouse Designs
(877) 372-1109
www.treehouse-designs.com
Tsukineko®, Inc.
(800) 769-6633
www.tsukineko.com
Tumblebeasts Stickers
(505) 323-5554
www.tumblebeasts.com
Two Busy Moms- see Deluxe Designs
USArtQuest
(800) 200-7848
www.usartquest.com
Victoria Art Supply- no contact info available
VIP Cranston Prints- no contact info available
Wal-Mart
www.walmart.com
Walnut Hollow®
(800) 950-5101
www.walnuthollow.com
Weekend Cropper
(586) 945-3282
www.weekendcropper.com
Welkmart- no contact info available
Westrim® Crafts
(800) 727-2727
www.westrimcrafts.com
Windsor & Newton- no contact info available
Wintech International Corp.
(800) 263-6043
www.wintechint.com
Wordsworth Stamps
(719) 282-3495
www.wordsworthstamps.com
Wrights- no contact info available

Index